FINANCIALLY EMPOWERED

ACHIEVING SUCCESS
THROUGH SACRIFICE

TERRANCE M. BACCHUS

ISBN 978-0-578-64868-2

Cover Design/Graphic: Streetlight Graphics
Author: Terrance M. Bacchus
Editor: DeeJan Copyediting & Proofreading Service
Printed in USA by Rehoboth Publishing, LLC

Disclaimer:
This work is not intended, and should not be construed, as a substitute for professional financial advice. The author does not hold himself out as a professional financial consultant, financial planner, or securities broker. This work is intended only as encouragement to the reader to explore and consider ways of thinking about the way they handle their money, based on the author's personal experience. Any advice on how to spend and where to invest should be sought from a qualified and licensed (where appropriate) professional.

CONTENTS

Foreword   v

Acknowledgments   xi

Preface   1

Introduction   5

1.   The American Dream   11

2.   Have No Excuses   21

3.   Empowered Living   26

4.   Education and the Pursuit of Happiness   36

5.   Motivated and Boston Strong   55

6.   Personal Accountability   68

7.   Obtain Wealth, Not Debt   75

8.   Wise Spending   82

9.   Equity and Wealth   97

10. Responsibility to Give Back   106

11. Emphasis On Social Media   113

12. Decisions, Decisions, Decisions   117

13. Just Be Disciplined   122

14. On Your Mark. Get Set. Invest.   127

15. Unexpected Emergency Preparation   132

16. Remember Your "Fun" Fund   141

17. No Lotto Tickets   147

18. Everything Society Has to Offer   152

19. You Are Ready For the Challenge   154

Bonus: Journey to Empowerment Starter Kit   158

FOREWORD

This writing is a living, occupational reward for me. Terrance was the first METCO (Metropolitan Council for Educational Opportunity, Inc.) student to sign up for, and remain in, the winter and spring track programs at Reading Memorial High School. This was in 1984. METCO was an inner-city program that brought black students to this mid-sized white community, eleven miles north of Boston. Their commute to Reading Memorial High School was approximately forty-five minutes each way, depending on traffic, which more than often was horrible. I was in my thirteenth year as coach of the teams, and we'd had a frustrating time trying to get METCO students on board. Race, scheduling and availability were the obstacles.

Seems to me that I became personally aware of Terrance on the first day of school or sometime that week in 1984, his sophomore year. He was easily recognized as a METCO student in Reading. I was an English teacher, and it was my habit to stand outside my second-floor door to watch the students passing to their next class. Terrance was among them daily. I recollect that he was solitary, silent and steady as he passed to whichever class. That fall, we became accustomed to saying hello and making small talk. We talked about school, sports, health and weather, and as winter approached, we spoke of track and field. Terrance, or "Tee" as he was familiarly known, had thought out the situation himself and signed up a few days before Thanksgiving.

The METCO bus, which left for Boston thirty minutes after school closed, was just one issue Tee would cope with throughout the next two and a half school years. Just one of the obstacles he would encounter and overcome with private sacrifice and persistence in his high school years. Several others, even more serious, he would carry himself. None of these were ever used as excuses in school or Reading track matters. He became a leader (captain of both the boys winter and spring track teams, 1986). Tee moved through those years with a facility for learning and communication. He accrued his own brand of social, intellectual and athletic success. Walking through the school, he exuded a genuine delight with and for others. Tee's innate happiness obviously made it easier to grapple with grim struggles beyond high school; confronting those obstacles was Tee's intuitive approach to not just surviving but thriving. Thus, thriving became his strongest weapon in overcoming adversity.

Hal Croft
Reading Memorial High School
Boys' Track and Field Coach: 1972 – 2014

"Success begins with sacrifice."

— Terrance Bacchus

ACKNOWLEDGMENTS

The process of completing this book taught me the meaning of what it is to truly wait on God. I was ready for this book to be completed nearly two years ago. I'm a results-oriented, get-the-job-done kind of guy. I despise procrastination of any sort and loathe unnecessary delays in both my personal and professional life. However, as I experience more of life, I am becoming acutely aware of the many things I cannot control, and God's will is at the top of that list. God doesn't work on our timeline, and it wasn't until He ordained my book to come to pass that I was able to complete it. In the process of finishing the book, I was reminded of a quip by the illustrious movie director, Woody Allen: *"If you want to make God laugh, tell Him about your plans."*

Now that the book is complete, I have a host of people I must acknowledge for their contributions and positive influences in my life. First and foremost, I want to acknowledge my mother. Mom, you taught me so much about the value of hard work. Raising three boys, Herbert "Herbie", Tom "Scoop", and me, was no small feat. You displayed remarkable strength and resiliency raising us on your own as a single mother. Your determination to ensure we had every opportunity to succeed and earn a great education is commendable. You were focused on our future and enrolled us in the METCO program in Reading, Massachusetts' school district. It was there I received my grade school education, which ultimately helped me fulfill my dream of attending Bentley College (now Bentley University).

As of the last census in 2010, the town of Reading had a population that was just under 1 percent African-American. It was even less than that back in the 1980s when I was a student. I share these statistics with you not to imply that racism and bigotry was an underlying reason for the absence of African-Americans or that people of color were not welcome in the town, but purely as a looking glass through which to gain insight into the environment I faced as a little inner-city boy beginning his educational journey.

During my time in Reading I met some amazing people who left a lasting impact on my life. The Valentine family was probably the most impactful. My relationship started with them in the first grade. Here I was, a stranger walking into their home, yet they welcomed me with open arms. Right away the family showed me unconditional love. The Valentines made me feel part of their family. They taught me that love is colorless. Dick Valentine, the head of the household, was a father figure to me. I learned some valuable lessons about manhood by watching him interact with his family. These wonderful people, who invested in me and my future, opened my eyes to a world that I never knew existed, and helped propel me into a life of prosperity.

Another key person from Reading was Mr. Hal Croft, my high school track coach. Mr. Croft is somewhat of a local legend. Not only was he a great coach, he served as the mentor I needed at that time of my life. Great coaching and committed mentoring have the capacity to bring the best out of you. Mr. Croft had those abilities. He was a special man who taught me two powerful lessons: first, how to use my God-given talent, and second, to be accountable for my own success. Those two valuable lessons prevented me from allowing myself to develop a victim mentality, no matter the situation I confronted. Mr. Valentine and Mr. Croft, thank you both for teaching me how to be a man of integrity, and for instilling the importance of helping others.

To Deloris, my college sweetheart, wife and mother of my daughters, I cannot thank you enough for always ensuring that we put God first, above all things. Thank you for your unwavering honesty, love, support and friendship. But most of all, thank you for presenting to me God's greatest gift, salvation. As a child, my mother introduced me to God, but you led me to Christ and helped me develop a relationship with Him that transformed my life and changed me forever. Together we have already achieved so much, and I believe the best is yet to come. I love you today, tomorrow, always and forever.

To my two beautiful daughters, Jasmine and Janae, I am so humbled to be your dad. You make me feel like the most blessed man on earth. Your compassion for humanity never ceases to amaze me. You both work very hard to achieve greatness and have hearts of gold when it comes to helping others. You two are the true inspiration that led me to help young people.

Family is the most important thing to me; good friends are a very close second. There is an old Irish proverb, *"A good friend is like a four-leaf clover: hard to find, lucky to have."* I am extremely grateful for some trusted friends who support, invest and believe in me. I treasure our relationships and never take them for granted. I want to thank Tony Leake, my best man. Back in the day, we were known as "TNT". I also want to thank Kèvin Cobb, my most loyal and trusted colleague, John Goetz, my good friend and close neighbor, and my Reading METCO family. Thank you all for real friendships of accountability.

To Tim Senff, my Crossroads Church Community Pastor, you are an amazing man of God. I am honored to serve under your leadership. Thank you for being a spiritual mentor and advisor in my life. Thank you for always being available when I need someone to talk to. Your encouragement and wise counsel have helped enrich my life.

Last, but certainly not least, this book would not have been written if it were not for my cousin, Richard Carrington II. Rich is more like a brother than a cousin and knows me better than most. It was his strong memory, with vivid details of our childhood and adolescence and shared stories, that helped make this collaboration successful. Love you, Cousin!

PREFACE

A s a boy, I dreamed one day I would become wealthy and successful. I didn't know exactly how it would happen; I just knew it would. During my college years, I felt myself getting closer to realizing that dream and achieving my goals. At the time, my focus was on graduating, getting a good job and accumulating a lot of money, as opposed to gaining or obtaining real wealth. I didn't understand the difference, until I started earning a salary and learned about saving and investing. I became financially literate and understood the true use of money and how to make it work for me. Too many people hope, wish and even pray for wealth and riches, yet their actions and spending habits say quite the contrary. People behaving recklessly with money is something I've seen too many

1

times. I know of a million big spenders whose eyes and appetites are bigger than their wallets. Regrettably, I predicted their negative outcomes. Some of those same people are still waiting on a savior to rescue them from financial bondage. They that continue to wait do so in vain.

On the contrary, those who are willing to take action and make the necessary changes have the opportunity to become financially empowered and obtain wealth. It's not an easy process, and many people never reach financial security, never mind financial success.

I was inspired to be an agent of change to help empower those whose backgrounds were similar to mine and anyone else looking to gain financial success. I want you to experience the same freedom that I have. I want you to avoid the dry desert of not enough and instead reside in the lush oasis of more than enough. Jesus said, *"I have come that you might have life and that more abundantly."* He didn't say, I come that you might struggle financially all your life and live under the heavy burden of debt. Every family needs some amount of wealth for economic security. It's my desire that as you read my story you will be inspired to become financially empowered; that you will adopt some techniques and suggestions, trim the fat out of your financial life through sacrifice, and ultimately achieve success.

INTRODUCTION

A college education is all but required to flourish in the current labor market, establish financial stability and build wealth. Research shows that college graduates earn $1 million more than high school graduates over their lifetime. As you advance in degrees, such as a masters or doctorate, the income gap doubles to $2 million and upwards. The correlation between education and financial success is undeniable. Still, the gap in college attainment by Whites versus Blacks and Latinos has widened over the last decade. I'm not sure if my mom had the data confirming these figures back when I was a child; nonetheless, she believed education was the key to living a prosperous life.

I am so grateful she had the forethought and courage that allowed me to participate in Met-

5

ropolitan Council for Educational Opportunity busing program, also known as METCO. I believe that single decision was a game-changer, which gave me the foundation to excel in college and a great underpinning for my personal life and professional career. The METCO program had that big of an impact in my life. The life lessons and relationships I developed throughout my years in METCO truly helped mold and shape me into the man I am today.

It was a not-for-profit, educational organization that primarily partnered with local suburban communities to place inner-city kids into suburban schools. Its mission was to provide students with a strong academic foundation rich in cultural, educational, ethnic, socioeconomic and racial diversity. It fostered the opportunity for children from Boston, and those from neighboring suburbs, to develop a deeper understanding of each other in an integrated public school setting.

For many years, Boston's inner-city schools were considered inferior. The graduation rates were atrocious. The schools were dangerous, underperforming pipelines that led kids from high school to low-wage jobs, prisons and lives of poverty. METCO was formed as part of a response to address some of those issues. Local community activists got together with caring and concerned families from the suburbs and agreed that change needed to happen. They felt that creating opportunities for inner-city children to attend better-performing schools in the suburbs would be a win-win endeavor. Cultures would learn from one another; barriers such as bigotry and prejudice could be replaced with inclusiveness and respect.

It was brilliant in theory; however, it wasn't all peaches and cream when it came to implementation. Like any program that challenges the status quo, there were drawbacks and unintended consequences. Some suburban towns were more resistant than others. I think the parents, more so than the students, were the most uncomfortable with our presence. They didn't feel we should be coming into their town and infringing on their way of life. We were not in any physical danger, but sometimes we faced verbal aggression.

METCO was a great blessing, yet my participation in the program required me to make major sacrifices even at a young age. While most kids at my age were still sleeping in their warm beds in the comfort of their homes, I was up and out walking to catch a bus, sometimes before dawn. At one point in elementary school I had to get up at 5:30 a.m. and walk almost two miles to catch the bus. While at school, I had to do whatever it took to fit in. I had to learn the ways and mores of the Reading students. I developed chameleon-like qualities that enabled me to fit in with my white counterparts. Then, when I was back home in my community, I had to switch back to the "Tee" my family and friends knew. I had to make sure they didn't think I was "acting White", a mindset that came from misunderstanding, and in some instances, plain jealousy. It was a major balancing act learning to straddle the two worlds. Sometimes it was almost like living a double identity.

But in the final analysis, there was tremendous value in my Reading METCO experience. There were more financial resources available in the Reading School District than in the inner-city. Two specific areas that stood out to me were guidance counselor support and sports. I had a

8

guidance counselor who went above and beyond to help me plan my future. My counselor met with me frequently and offered recommendations. She actually encouraged me to apply to Bentley College and provided assistance with filling out my application. This may not sound like much, but my friends back in my neighborhood didn't receive the same assistance and many of them weren't encouraged to apply to college. As a student athlete, I played football and participated in track and field. I not only had great coaches to support me, I also had access to probably the best high school outdoor track in the state of Massachusetts, whereas many of the inner-city schools in Boston were forced to share a track. To me it seemed that college recruiters focused more on the suburban schools for both admissions and student athlete recruitment. In my mind, my athletic talent got their attention, but the letter of recommendation from my guidance counselor sealed the deal. To be transparent, my grades weren't the best, so it was probably my athletic ability and that letter of recommendation that led to my admission to Bentley College. This ultimately resulted in me being the first person in my entire family to attend and graduate from college. My exposure to that world broadened my horizons and prepared me to maneuver in the corporate boardroom, while still being able to hold my own on the inner-city streets.

1

THE AMERICAN DREAM

Success and fulfillment are not gifts to be given, they are accomplishments that must be earned. Hip-hop preacher, Eric Thomas's philosophy about success is profound. He breaks it down like this: *"When you want to succeed as bad as you want to breathe, then you will be successful."* That may seem extreme to some, but I can relate to his position. I was consistently told you have to earn what you want in this life. When I was growing up, the older people used phrases like, *"It's a dog-eat-dog world"* and *"It's survival of the fittest."* That type of thinking may be considered passé now. Regardless, nobody is going to just hand you the keys to success. Success comes at a cost. What are you willing to sacrifice for your financial success?

Throughout history, purpose-driven dream chasers have made great sacrifices to attain wealth and riches. They have given up decades of their lives and terminated intimate and important relationships as well as any and everything that hindered their quest to fulfill goals. They maximized the time they were allotted in life. Time management, more specifically, effective time management, is a key factor for successful living. How you spend your twenty-four hours is an indication of where you are headed. Author Malcolm Gladwell says in his New York Times bestselling book, *Outliers,* that *"It takes roughly 10,000 hours of practice to achieve mastery in a field."* Your journey to financial success is no different. It's going to take that same amount of time, energy and commitment to the process in order to achieve financial success.

Today, we live in a society where every child gets a participation trophy just for being on the team. Be mindful, the real world doesn't operate in that manner. Adults don't get participation trophies. No matter how magnificent and special people have said you are, their kind words and encouragement can only take you so far. True purpose, fulfillment, happiness and destiny are your personal responsibilities. You have the right to live the best life you want and can afford. With that right comes the responsibility to do all that is required to attain it.

Wishing, hoping and dreaming will only take you so far. Don't spend too much time waiting for Publishers Clearing House to show up at your front door with an oversized check endorsed to you. Seven thousand dollars a week for life does sound pretty good, but you will probably have better luck finding the leprechaun's pot of gold at the end of a rainbow before that happens. If you truly want your piece of the American pie and financial success, be prepared to aggressively pursue it.

Pretty much everything in life that's worth having takes going after it. I learned that lesson at a young age. As a kid, I remember my mother would say at times, *"Tonight, dinner is every man for himself."* This was after a long day at work and she didn't feel like cooking. If you wanted to eat, you had to get up and go fix dinner yourself. Hopefully, you didn't lollygag around too long until there was nothing left. If I just sat around waiting for someone to bring it to me, I would have gone to bed on an empty stomach. And she wouldn't have had any sympathy for me. She would have hit me with one of her favorite sayings, *"That's too bad for you."* It was her way of teaching us to be independent and self-sufficient. It worked.

When I think about my journey and where I'm at today, I can harken back to sitting in my high school social studies class learning about *"The American Dream."* The way my teachers presented the concept, it seemed relatively easy to attain if I heeded their instructions. Prosperity, happiness and the fullness of life were all mine for the taking. I could really be the successful businessman I envisioned. All I had to do was go to school, work hard, follow the rules, and I too could have my piece of The American Dream. That was a great message to a kid like me growing up in the inner city. They were showing me the way to success, leading me down the road to empowerment and financial independence. That was my way out, so I was all ears. My reward for following their instructions was the nice home in the suburbs with a pretty white picket fence, the

2.5 kids and the desires of my heart. However, it wasn't quite that simple.

While the teachers did a pretty good job of motivating us, they rarely mentioned the great sacrifices involved in the process of obtaining financial wealth. They presented the process in a broad and macro fashion. But it's the micro, day-to-day, week-to-week and year-to-year sacrifices, that make the difference. There is an old saying, *"The devil is in the details."* Thankfully, I'm a detail-oriented person. I went out and found the information that the teachers left out.

When I was coming up in the 1980s, teachers were a little different. Social media wasn't around, so they did not have that challenge to face. Teachers back then were not nearly as friendly as teachers are today. They even had a different outlook on bullies and what they called tattletales. Not to say they encouraged any type of bad behavior or physical fighting, but you can't tell me they didn't know kids were fighting outside in the back after school. They allowed kids to work out a lot of issues on their own. Really, all they wanted was for you to succeed. They didn't hand you anything, although sometimes they invested a little more into you, if they saw you were not living up to your potential. Still, you had to earn your grades. They wanted you to succeed and move on. So they drilled that mantra of working hard into our heads. We were taught to love our country, and every morning we pledged allegiance to our flag. America, the land of the free and the home of the brave, was known as the great melting pot where people near and far were willing to sacrifice their lives to get a chance at that wonderful dream.

My love for this country burns in my heart. But I learned very early in grade school that there were two Americas or at least different versions of American reality for me. There was a reality that many of my white classmates in Reading enjoyed, and a completely different reality that the majority of METCO kids who were bused to Reading endured. Those realities were too difficult for some METCO students to handle because they were anything but subtle. There were stark, vivid distinctions that not only separated us but challenged the self-esteem and self-worth of some kids. As a result, some kids left on their own and dealt with the Boston Public Schools, while other kids were asked to leave by the school. But for those in my class who overcame all of the obstacles and found a way to excel, it was worth the challenge.

For me, it opened my eyes and showed me another version of what life could be. Yet it didn't change the reality I faced. One reality was set in the nice classrooms of the middle-class suburban school I attended. The other version was eleven miles down the road, which I saw when I got off the school bus at the corner of my street in the inner-city. When I looked out the giant windows of my classroom, I saw some beautiful homes with bright white picket fences. I saw big, blossoming trees and beautifully landscaped yards. On the other hand, when I looked outside my bedroom window, I saw something completely different. I saw an abundance of kids playing street football and hide-and-go-seek in abandoned buildings. I saw wild dogs and stray cats fighting for scraps out of the dumpster behind the corner store. I saw rows of brick apartment buildings with big black iron bars on the windows. Worst of all, at a young age, I was aware of community members being murdered. It was because of God's grace

I didn't suffer from PTSD. I didn't see a lot of prosperity or people living The American Dream I learned about in school.

As I further reflect, what I saw as I looked out my window was the cold, harsh reality that so many inner-city kids see today. I saw lower-middle class and poor people struggling to make ends meet. At times, I saw violence and crime and some people just up to no good. I saw single mothers carrying shopping bags from the supermarket and convenience stores. Every day I walked by the local drunks sitting at the bus stop or on the curb, drinking Wild Irish Rose or whatever dollar-bottle of fortified wine they could drink from a brown paper bag. It wasn't a pretty sight, and the smell was even worse. It was commonplace for young risk-takers to do things that would land them in jail and cost them their freedom. Their desperation and ignorance wouldn't allow them to see the true punishment for their behavior. They had no idea how those poor choices would haunt them throughout life. They were lost at a young age. But that was the reality of the place I called home. Hopelessness and despair were ever before me, trying to penetrate my spirit and draw me into their dark clouds.

Despite all of the negativity I witnessed, I was able to find the silver lining. Plus, I had some successful examples to look to for inspiration. Boston is home to one of the greatest R&B groups of all time, New Edition. They grew up in my neighborhood, and I saw them work tirelessly to perfect their craft. The group's dedication to achieving their goals was inspiring. I witnessed them going from competing at local talent shows to performing at the Grammys. They were living examples of hard work paying off. Seeing the results of their hard work firsthand motivated me to go after my dreams.

There were other local people I watched go after their dreams. One of my friends, Wyatt, was a great dancer involved in the performing arts. He had incredible discipline for his craft. His hard work led to amazing success. He traveled around the world performing and living out his dreams. Those success stories were few and far between, but they served as glimmers of hope.

What I observed from my bedroom window I never saw myself being a part of. I was in that world, but I was not of that world. I was a sojourner in my neighborhood, an ambitious and friendly traveler making my way through. Please

19

don't misunderstand me. I'm not ashamed of where I came from. In fact, I'm proud; it contributed to making me a strong-willed overcomer. Besides, it was just one stop in my pursuit of happiness. I had imagination, vision and determination, and I believed that one day I would live The American Dream we studied. The one I witnessed from the windows of my school in Reading. The one that included some of the nicest homes I'd ever set foot in and cars I had ever ridden in.

I believe individuals are only limited by their imagination. I'm from the school of faith and positive thinking. The one that says, *"If you can believe it, you can achieve it."* And that's not just a slogan, it's a belief system that helped shape me and created many successful millionaires. My beliefs allowed me to take on all obstacles and barriers that were in front of me, so that one day I would live my best life. But I could only accomplish my goals through singleness of purpose, a relentless pursuit of what I wanted, and a willingness to sacrifice everything that was required for my success and financial independence.

2

HAVE NO EXCUSES

We live in a world of abundant excuses. Quite frankly, excuses are often used as cop outs or reasons to justify one's failure. Behavioral scientist, Steve Maraboli says, *"We may place blame, give reasons, and even have excuses; but in the end, it is an act of cowardice to not follow your dreams."* As you push forward in your life, I caution you to resist the temptation to offer excuses if you truly want to be successful in your finances and every other area of your life. Excuses are a safe place to rest for the unsatisfied and underachieving. They are a soft landing spot for those who fail to reach their goals and look for a way out of personal responsibility. In my opinion, successful people do not offer or accept excuses. In fact, throughout history, some of the most successful people had a disdain for excuse-making. For example, Florence Nightingale said, *"I attribute my success to this: I never gave or took any excuse."* That's some of the best free advice I have ever heard. Then there is the late Kobe Bryant, whom I was not the biggest fan of. Yet I acknowledge his basketball greatness and business expertise. He once said, *"I have nothing in common with lazy people who blame others for their lack of success. Great things come from hard work and perseverance. No Excuses."* Are you seeing the theme? Excuses are not acceptable! Just as Kobe was focused on becoming one of the greatest NBA players of all time, we must strive to obtain our own level of greatness.

I'm not naïve; not everyone is willing to do what it takes to achieve greatness. Some lack the discipline and stick-to-itiveness it takes to reach those goals. Now, I will stop short of calling anyone shiftless or lazy, although there are a number of people who don't necessarily work hard enough to reach their potential. They look everywhere but in the mirror for someone to blame for their condition.

There is some evidence that excuse-making is passed down through generations. Parents have to be hypervigilant with their children when it comes to making excuses and, they have to do so at an early age. Kids come up with 101 excuses for why they don't complete their household chores or homework. When it comes to the latter, the old-time favorite is, *"The dog ate my homework."* I wonder how many kids who didn't have dogs used that one?

Children aren't the only ones guilty of using excuses; adults have had years to master the behavior. A big area where excuses are prevalent is places of employment. Over the years in my role as a manager and leader, I have heard a myriad of excuses as to why people didn't meet deadlines or sales goals. Sometimes the excuse was that they weren't given a realistic timeline. Other times, they pointed the finger at having a lack of resources. We live in a results-oriented society. If you can't produce at the level you are expected, most companies will look to replace you. As a leader I tried to encourage, motivate and challenge those I worked with to meet their goals, by assisting them any way I could. Many times I had to sacrifice family time in order to stay late at the office to help on projects.

I realize most excuses are based out of fear. The fear of failing, the fear of not being good enough, the fear of succeeding, the fear of being broke are all examples of excuses that hinder people from reaching their dreams. So many people have great business ideas, but the fear of branching out on their own keeps them from trying. Fear may be the biggest dream killer of all time. Having been the first person in my entire family to go to college, I had a fear of failing. What if I didn't graduate? What if I didn't get a good job? Despite my fears, I still worked hard and challenged myself to meet my goals.

In addition to excuse-making, its kissing cousin, the art of blame-shifting has reached an all-time high. I even heard someone refer to the time we are living in as the "blaming culture". Well, I'm here to tell you that if your child doesn't make the basketball team, don't blame the coach. It might be that the other players are more talented. Likewise, if your child receives a poor grade, it's easy to blame the teacher or professor. However, she may have earned a poor grade because she didn't study enough.

Every day, more and more people are surrendering their dreams and closing the door on expectations, only to succumb to the *"Woe is Me"* disposition. *"It isn't fair; the deck is stacked against me."* Racism, classism or some other "ism" is holding people back. Those obstacles are real setbacks and stumbling blocks that many people unfortunately face. Notwithstanding, they are not immovable objects. Knowledge, faith and determination can surmount them and allow you to soar above those hindrances. I faced many of them and, thankfully, I never fell into that self-pity mindset. I took responsibility for my destiny and accountability for my decisions. Yet, I understand how people can fall into that trap. Along my journey, I have taken my share of losses, bumps and bruises, some at the hands of an "ism." Still, I didn't sit by passively hoping things would get better. I overcame the challenges and fought for what I wanted. You must do the same. Sometimes the fight will not be fair, but that doesn't give us an excuse to quit fighting.

3

EMPOWERED LIVING

In the previous chapters, we discussed the overwhelming use of excuses and the victim mentality far too many members of society possess. We also discussed the presence of unbalanced playing fields. We came to the consensus that barriers, roadblocks and obstacles occur in life beyond our control, requiring us to adjust, manipulate or change our disposition. While the degrees of our individual challenges vary, none of us will escape life's difficulties on *"Flowery beds of ease."* Inescapably, all of us must endure unmerited heartache, pain, and disappointment in our lives. To add to the distress, biased systems are put in place that benefit some and hurt others. Still, we must persevere to reach our goals and dreams. The famous writer, William Penn, while in prison wrote one of his most poignant pieces, *No Cross, No Crown.* Written into this great country's precious Declaration of Independence is a very familiar and often quoted passage that states, "We hold these truths to be self-evident, that all men are created equal, that they are endowed by their Creator with certain unalienable Rights, which among these are Life, Liberty and the pursuit of Happiness." These famous words represent what's great about our country.

In contrast, there is a dark blemish that hovers over our beautiful democracy. Under the letter of the law all men are created equal. However, racial, ethnic, and socioeconomic disparities and other forces often tilt the fair, competitive conditions for people of color and other minorities in their pursuit of happiness. This is something far greater, and in a whole different atmosphere, than excuse-making and blame-shifting. There are major segments of our population that constantly fight a never-ending, uphill battle on roller skates for opportunities that are given to others. It's demoralizing and destructive to the personal psyche. Immoral obstacles and unscrupulous barriers have boxed out large numbers of society in their pursuit of The American Dream. One of the biggest examples was the systematic practice of American slavery, which nearly destroyed the African-American race. It's encouraging to finally hear a number of influential leaders acknowledge the devastation that occurred and admit to the racist practices that set the Black race back several decades. During the brutal and inhuman years that slavery was practiced, African-Americans were not able to pursue happiness, primarily because they spent nearly every waking hour just trying to survive. However, even in survival mode, some worked extra hours (if you can believe that!) and hired themselves out as contractors to other slave owners to earn income. Some earned so much money that they were able to buy their freedom. Some extraordinary people have done incredible things, and purchasing one's freedom was an amazing feat considering the circumstances. This could only be accomplished by people willing to sacrifice nearly everything to reach their goals. I don't equate my struggles and journey with those amazing people, but on a much smaller scale, I do equate my sacrifices. Although slavery officially ended in 1865, its devastating effects continued for several generations. Laws were passed to prevent African-Americans from owning property. They were denied basic human rights, such as voting and access to public education as well as equal treatment under the law. Moreover, the 40 acres and a mule that were promised when the south surrendered to the north never materialized. Instead, there were Jim Crow laws, redlining, and other discriminatory practices which created almost insurmountable barriers for people of color to prosper financially. So, any chance they had to start building wealth was pretty much impossible. Those are the cold, hard, ugly facts about this great country; that's the other side of The American Dream. Call it The American Nightmare. The remnants of these antiquated and barbaric practices still have a holdover effect today on society. Nevertheless, the strength, resiliency, and desire for a better life don't allow the story to end just like that. Again, I hearken back to the saying, *"If you can believe it, you can achieve it."*

29

Despite all those obstacles, some very amazing people, through discipline, hard work and good stewardship, were able to break through those barriers. Therefore, if the people who lived back then were able to excel under those horrendous conditions, I am confident that I, and anyone else who is committed to winning in this life, can and will overcome any obstacle that comes our way.

The right attitude is essential. I read somewhere that *"Your attitude determines your altitude."* Amy Ruley, former women's basketball coach at North Dakota State, said, *"Everyone wants to win, but I think winners believe they deserve to win. They've made the commitment, they've followed the right path, and they've taken the right steps to be successful."* This world is full of wonderful and amazing people who possess a positive attitude and a can-do spirit, who, every single day of the year, go out and win or prepare to win, by doing the things that are required. The world is also awash with complainers, excuse-makers and ne'er-do-well people who willfully submit their power, dreams and destiny to chance, ideology and ignorance.

30

I challenge you to rise above all the negativity and noise and join me in living the life we've dreamed of. If we are truly steadfast in our pursuit, nothing can prohibit us from reaching our goals. I want to inspire you to live a financially empowered life.

That said, you don't have to go it alone. I don't profess to have attained all of what I accomplished on my own. We all need people who are willing to invest in us, to bring their talent and wisdom to our lives, much like Mr. Croft poured his time and knowledge into me back in high school. Over the years, I've gained a lot of knowledge by watching and observing family members, mentors and others who were successful. They were not always the richest and shrewdest, but they were people who sacrificed tremendously to better their conditions and reach their goals. My mother taught me the most about the importance of making sacrifices. I remember her telling me at a very young age that I had to work twice as hard for the same grades, jobs and positions as my white counterparts. That was a big pill for a young child to swallow. It wasn't fair. It wasn't what they said in school. I was taught we were all created equal. Maybe that was just her experience growing up.

My mother grew up during the height of the Civil Rights movement where the racial climate was very real and in-your-face. Anybody who lived during those times, or studied them in school, can probably remember the police spraying fire hoses and unleashing attack dogs on innocent people who were protesting peacefully for equal rights and equal opportunities. That was a reality she lived firsthand. She grew up in a very different America than I did. She experienced being passed over for positions and promotions that she was more qualified for than the people who received them. For most people, any of those precarious situations could cause resentment, but my mother just persevered through it, understanding that the game was rigged. Saying the game was rigged may have sounded like an excuse or justification. It wasn't. It's factual, and we have more than a hundred years of documented proof.

In the face of all the bigotry and racism my mom experienced, she still persevered. My mother taught me to love everyone but be mindful of

32

the systemic issues that could possibly hinder me in my pursuit of The American Dream. I didn't fully understand what she meant at the time, but as I grew older and experienced more life, I learned. I felt it firsthand in high school, experiencing things that were not fair or equitable, and didn't feel good. Actually, it felt awful. I was purposely passed over for recognition and accolades that I not only deserved but earned through hard work and dedication. It hurt me to the core, but at the same time, it motivated me to work harder. I overcame those barriers and reached my goals, and in the end, I received the recognition that was justifiably due. When I got to college, I was completely aware or "woke", as they commonly say today, of how society truly operated. I had 20/20 vision when it came to recognizing the vast disparities and discrepancies of society, even before my Lasik surgery. Injustice has a way of opening your eyes.

One of my main objectives in writing this book was to empower people, much like myself, who grew up in single-parent families in the inner city. We may have a shared commonality and vision when it comes to dreams of financial success. Many of us know what it means to struggle. I also want to help those who may come from different backgrounds and different stages of life who are looking to obtain wealth. Collectively, we are one, yearning for a better life for our families, our children and our children's children. But for any of us to leave a financial legacy, we must be willing to work smart and hard. So right now, do me a favor. Ask yourself, "What am I willing to do and what am I willing to give up for financial empowerment and success?" It comes with a price. Sometimes that price is so steep that people are not willing to pay it. As for me, I made a sacrifice the day I entered the workforce. My dream was to one day live in a house and have the freedom to retire early. Thus, making a commitment to invest in a retirement plan and save for a home were my first priorities.

Each of us has an individual journey to take in the pursuit of happiness. Whatever road you decide to take, it requires sacrifice. And remember, the greater the sacrifice the greater the reward. The bottom line is that, regardless of real or perceived obstacles and overwhelming barriers, you absolutely have the ability to achieve real financial success.

True personal sacrifice, relentless hard work, discipline and stewardship over your money, which includes saving and investing, will position you for success. Follow me, as I share my personal journey and challenge you to walk along your own road to financial success.

4

EDUCATION AND THE PURSUIT OF HAPPINESS

Financial success is not coming to look for you. You can be the nicest person in the world and do all the wishing you want. But until you commit to doing whatever is required to prosper financially, you will simply be spinning your wheels and wasting your energy. Yes, we have inalienable rights in our pursuit of happiness, but those rights don't come with any guarantees. You have to possess a burning desire that is unable to be quenched by anything less than your goals. You have to make a concerted effort to go after it and be willing to make the countless necessary sacrifices to achieve it.

In my case, I was passionate about obtaining financial success by any means necessary. That may sound a little bit dramatic, but it's the truth.

I was determined not to allow negative thinking, negative people or negative situations stop me from reaching my goal of financial success. In a world full of detractors and doomsayers, I remained focused on my vision.

Before I go any further, I think it's important to clarify my passion for financial success and wealth. I was not obsessed with obtaining or amassing money but rather with the things I could do with the money. I don't consider myself to be a shallow or shortsighted person. My goals and dreams extend well beyond my ability to purchase nice houses and fancy cars. My aim for financial success was to be able to leave a legacy for my children and their children. Creating generational wealth, like the Kennedys and other wealthy families who left fortunes for their heirs, was the objective. The late Joe Kennedy left millions for his children and future generations. They could live off the interest of the money he left, even if they never worked a day in their lives. Imagine being able to leave a couple million dollars to your children, who are then able to live off the interest alone. Would that type of wealth be a game-changer for your family? I know it would be for mine. That's the type of generational wealth I have spent the last thirty years trying to create and preserve. It is important that I ensure no one in my lineage would ever experience poverty or suffer financial hardship. That being said, my wife and I set out to teach our daughters the value of a good education and a strong work ethic. While they grew up enjoying more financial resources than some other families, we made a conscious effort to avoid giving them everything they wanted. Instead, we practiced discipline and diligently worked to foster a sense of gratefulness and humility. It was important that they be aware of the complexities of society and the racial and socioeconomic inequalities that can affect one's personal financial decisions. In addition, we taught them the importance of setting goals for themselves, and most importantly, having a relationship with God. They needed to know that with God's help they could accomplish anything they wanted.

I am passionate about closing the racial wealth gap that exists today. I've read that less than 2% of African American families have a net worth of $1 million dollars compared to 15% for

White families. There is a huge opportunity to close this gap, and my wife and I are in the process of building our own financial legacy to help do this.

Now, having said this, anything can happen in life. We could experience a national tragedy and the stock market could crash again. My company could decide to terminate my employment. Any number of financial issues can arise, but I don't want the fallout to affect my children. That's why I'm making fiscal preparations now. I've used every resource available to me to create a financial working plan or blueprint. And more importantly, I'm executing my plan and continuously improving it. There are thousands, if not millions, of people who had great plans and blueprints, but when the time came to execute them, they were unable to do so. As a result, their plans did not prosper. A plan alone is just grandiose words on paper, until you implement it.

Coming up, the older people told us, *"Actions speak louder than words."* People can say anything; the world is full of big talkers. There are plenty of charismatic and motivational people who are available to help you reach your personal and financial goals, each with their own agenda. As for me, I'm your resource with impeccable integrity, here to coach you. My only agenda is to help you create wealth. I'm sharing my story to motivate you. And all I want is for you to win. That's right, win. Win the game of financial success. Some individuals charge a fee, which can be very expensive. Financial advisors are some of the highest-paid people. You place your hard-earned money into their care, and hope and pray that they manage it honestly and live up to their fiduciary responsibilities. Often, if you don't have a lot of money to manage, they won't pay a lot of attention to you. Also keep in mind that in any field there are some people you can trust and others who are untrustworthy, so you have to do the research. A very small number of people will help you out of the kindness of their hearts; those are few and far between. When it comes to free advice, remember the old saying, *"You get what you pay for."* Whatever direction you choose to follow, there is an abundance of information on the web. Armchair financial gurus and "wannabe" analysts are available to you online. You still have to do the work. It requires discipline and a willingness to sacrifice to get what you want.

Thinking back to when I was young, I don't recall hearing the terms, "motivational speaker" or "financial guru." We didn't have Tony Robbins, Wayne Dyer or Les Brown. Zig Ziglar was around, but not on my radar. My influencers were my mother, my teachers and a few successful men I knew in Reading. My mother's mantra was to go to school and get a good education. She believed, like many people, that education would solve it all. My teachers told me I could be anything I wanted to be if I studied hard and applied myself. A good teacher or coach can inspire and motivate you to move mountains. However, with all the inspiration they gave, they never specifically talked about financial success. I guess we just assumed that with a good job we would make a lot of money. The process of making and increasing money was never really addressed. There were very few, if any, classes on financial literacy. It wasn't the school's responsibility to teach that; it was left up to the parents. Consequently, if you didn't come from a wealthy or upwardly mobile middle-class family, the only thing you knew about money was that your family didn't have enough. It wasn't until I got to college and started taking business classes that I began to learn in-depth about finances. Hitherto, my mom and teachers served as my motivators because I believed what they told me. But to tell you the truth, my neighborhood was all the motivation I needed.

Growing up in inner-city Boston, none of my friends had much money. A couple of my friends' parents owned homes, but that was about it. Notwithstanding, the lack of money didn't stop us from dreaming of one day being wealthy and successful. I knew I would have to work hard because no one was going to give me anything. The great Sam Cooke's hit song, *"The Best Things in Life Are Free," is a classic,* but I'm not sure I completely agree with his premise. It takes money and resources to live the life I'm planning. Love is free, a family is sometimes free and friendships are free. However, none of those things pay the mortgage or our daughters' college tuitions. Sometimes the best things in life are *not* free. But maybe the freedom comes with having the ability to pay for everything you need and desire.

As kids, we would have conversations and fantasize about how our lives were going to be when we got older and pursued our careers. We all had big plans. I hung around dreamers and go-getters. Some of us wanted to be lawyers, others business owners and corporate executives. Dick Valentine, my host parent, worked in corporate America, and I wanted to be just like him. He was very successful and a great provider for his family. He inspired me. He was one of the reasons I went to Bentley College to study business. I knew it would prepare me to be a professional like him. Anyway, my friends and I were young and ambitious, and nothing was going to stop us.

I dreamed of living in a big house and driving a fancy sports car. We all had our favorite cars. One of my friends wanted a Corvette Stingray and another wanted a Ferrari. I wanted the Pontiac Firebird Trans Am, like the one from *Smokey and the Bandit*, one of my all-time favorite movies. That black and gold muscle car, driven by the late Burt Reynolds, was something to behold. I could picture myself behind the steering wheel, driving that thing on the highway with a beautiful young lady in the passenger seat and the T-tops down. We allowed our imaginations to take us to the places we wanted to go. As I said, I didn't know how I was going to get there, I just knew I would make it. Some of us were too naïve to think it wasn't possible to achieve what we wanted. We had no idea we were low-income kids, because all of us pretty much had the same amount of stuff.

Summer vacations some years consisted of both day and overnight camps, if you were able to get into them. They were free or cost very little money, so slots ran out quickly. Boston College had a great sports day camp facilitated by the basketball team. It was all-day fun, and they fed you breakfast, lunch and a snack. There was some instruction time, but you mostly ran all day. By the time you got home, you were exhausted. Then there were overnight camps geared toward city kids, sponsored by Morgan Memorial Goodwill and the Salvation Army. I went a couple of times, but I wasn't a big fan. I liked being home at night and sleeping in my own bed.

When we were not at camp, we would spend all day at the Metropolitan District Commission

(MDC) city pool. My friends and I would gather there in the morning and usually stay until it closed, especially on those really hot summer days. When we were not at the pool we played outside at the basketball courts or on the fields from morning until night. We would walk to different neighborhoods in the city and challenge other kids to football and basketball games. We always found something to do. We were never idle – that was the devil's playground. My close friends and I fled from trouble and anything that could jeopardize our way of life.

Some of the neighborhood kids were stealing cars and getting into all kinds of other mischief, but we never felt any pressure to join in. We did silly stuff like crank calling. I remember we would look through the phone book and pick out random numbers, call them and pretend to be a staff person from Sears department store. Our line would be, "Is your refrigerator running?" And when they answered, "Yes", we would say, "Well you better go catch it." That was the kind of harmless mischief we would get into.

Probably the worst thing we did was to "AB" a few cabs. For those of you who don't know what

"AB" is, it's when you take a taxicab to a location, and when the cab stops at the red light, you jump out and run away without paying. I never knew exactly what "AB" stood for. All I knew was that I always got stuck in the middle seat because I was the fastest runner. They used to call me "Carl Lewis" (U.S. gold medal sprinter). I channeled him every time I jumped out of a cab. It was stupid and, thank God, we never got caught. We had a couple of close calls, but no driver was going to leave his cab alone in our neighborhood to chase after us.

When we were old enough to work we got summer jobs from ABCD, the local anti-poverty group that helped inner city kids and families. Those jobs were fun and didn't require us to work too hard. When I was blessed to go places in the summer, it was usually one of the amusement parks in the area, or one of the local beaches. Nantasket Beach, one of my favorites, was nice. They had fried dough and fun carnival games. It was only a few miles of a drive from my house, but it was like going on vacation for a day. We didn't go a lot, but the times we did were great. Those were some of the best times of my youth.

Kids today, especially my children, would laugh at what we considered treats. We thought taking the ride down American Legion Highway to McDonald's, standing in line and ordering whatever we wanted, was a big deal. My favorites were the Big Mac, french fries and vanilla shake. That's no big deal today; some kids go to McDonald's once a week or more. But at that time it was a sacrifice for my mom. She had to save up to feed our family of four. I might be waxing nostalgic, but the times have really changed in just one generation. We lived simple, humble, typical, inner-city kids' lives. Don't get me wrong. I don't believe any of us was living below the poverty line. We never went to bed hungry or worried about where our next meal was coming from. My mother ensured we had everything we needed when it came to food and shelter. Nonetheless, things were very limited.

Once in a while, she splurged on items like the floor model color television. When I was growing up, a floor model color television was a luxury and not many people in the inner city had them. Nowadays, nearly every house in the United States has at least two or three large flat-screen televisions. Even though there were times when my mom had a little extra money to splurge, we experienced some real struggles and sometimes things were tight. There was not a lot of spare cash hanging around in the family's passbook savings account. My mother saved what she could, but a lot of times her check was already spent before she got it.

In addition, I would be remiss if I didn't acknowledge the fact that while we were never on welfare or public assistance, I did have my share of government cheese and some of the other non-labeled agricultural products, like peanut butter, which was routinely provided to lower-income families. A lot of you reading this book have no idea what I am talking about and may need to reference Google. But those who grew up during that time can confirm that the peanut butter was okay if you used it right away. Now, it wasn't the Skippy brand, which was the smoothest and best back in the day, but the government peanut butter did the trick when you ran out of the good stuff. Although, after it had been sitting in the cabinet for a while, it would congeal into a hard block and was difficult to spread, causing you to rip apart one of your slices of Wonder Bread as you attempted to make a PB&J sandwich. But it had a decent taste to it, and if it was all you had, you made it work. It just might be the reason PB&J is my favorite sandwich today. Overall, those government food products filled in the gaps for many families when household food supplies got low.

On the other hand, where I drew the line was with the nonfat powdered milk. I couldn't get with a big white box with black lettering that just said, "Powdered Milk". There was just something not right about adding water to an instant powder to make milk. We learned as little children that milk came from cows and goats, not a box. We went on school trips to dairy farms and learned to milk cows. Today we get milk from almonds, cashews, coconuts and a host of different products. The concept of adding water to powder was completely foreign. Thousands of families did it, and I didn't sit in judgment about it because people in my family did it, too, but I couldn't do it. I guess in life you have to draw the line somewhere. It's also the reason I hate milk today. My mother, and everyone else, would say it almost tasted the same as the regular whole milk if you let it get really cold. They knew that wasn't the truth, and my taste buds did too, but hey, what were they going to say? I couldn't stand the stuff, and there was no way I was eating my Frankenberry cereal and Apple Jacks with that instant milk stuff. So when we were out of milk, I didn't eat cereal.

The government products weren't all bad. Some of the best macaroni and cheese I ever tasted was made from the big block of government cheese that we received. My mother knew how to work with those products, and she did the very best she could with the resources she had. They say, *"Necessity is the mother of invention."* You figure out ways to make things work for you. My mother's limited money had to stretch a long way. As a result, less expensive meats, like chicken, were my mother's main go-to. Every now and then my mother would go down to Carl and Eddie's Meat Market and purchase some thick, center-cut pork chops. She would season and fry them, and then serve them with some rice and veggies. Sometimes she would smother them in homemade gravy and they would be so tender they would melt in your mouth. This was way before a lot of people were concerned about eating pork. Besides, in my mother's house you ate what was on your plate or, by your own choice, you wouldn't eat.

That was our reality. After working all day and coming home to cook for us, she expected no complaints. You ate what she cooked and you liked it. It wasn't a problem for me because I liked just about everything my mother cooked. And what I didn't like I kept to myself because, if she thought I had a problem, she would cook it purposely. Ever had liver and onions? It wasn't the tastiest meal, but when you were hungry you could make believe it was steak, though when you bit into it you knew it wasn't.

Anyway, my mother was blessed with the ability to take a few simple ingredients and turn them into a spectacular meal. One of her specialties was spaghetti with her homemade meat sauce. Sometimes I watched, as she would cut up those green peppers and onions and then sauté them in her favorite cast-iron frying pan that had lost a lot of its shine and looked like it had been handed down a couple of generations.

Then she would mix in some ground beef we got from the big market (Haymarket Square in downtown Boston).

I have to digress for a moment to tell you about the big market because it was such an important part of my childhood. The big market had great bargains and only opened on Saturdays. It was the place where you could get the biggest bang for your buck (and we didn't have many bucks to work with). When I was growing up, there were no Walmart Supercenters, Target retail stores, or Costco Wholesale stores in our neighborhood. We had neighborhood supermarkets and "mom and pop" corner stores that were so expensive your money couldn't go far. Ever heard the term, *"highway robbery"?* Going to those stores was exactly that! Therefore, we would wake up early on Saturday mornings, catch the local bus to the orange-line subway station and trek to the big market. The place opened at 6 a.m. We sacrificed sleeping in, so we could get there early and get the best deals. Also, if we were good and mom had money left over, she would buy us a slice of pizza. It may be revisionist history, but I haven't had pizza that good since Haymarket, and believe me, I'm a pizza connoisseur.

Anyhow, let's get back to my mom's recipe. She would add her secret spices and a giant can of tomato sauce to her spaghetti and magic was created. But the pièce de résistance came once you added a little of that grated parmesan cheese blend in the tall, thin blue box. At that point you were experiencing the best spaghetti you ever tasted. I've traveled all around this fine country and have eaten at some of the finer dining establishments, and I can honestly say that none of their spaghetti and meat sauce dishes have come close to my mother's recipe.

Somebody might say, *"What's the big deal?"* Well, as I look back over my life, I have a greater appreciation for the sacrifices my mother made. I really don't know how she did it. Having to clothe and feed my brothers and me on a very modest salary was surely difficult and required creativity and serious financial discipline. I honor those sacrifices she made, for they were the underpinning of my success. I thank her for the scrappy, never-give-up Boston attitude she passed down to me. I have spent my life making sacrifices, finding or creating the best deals and making strategic choices that have helped me get to where I am today. That's why I can proudly say that there is no shame in my game. Although I currently reside in Ohio, I will forever be Boston Strong, so much so that it's the slogan on the license plate of my car.

5

Motivated and Boston Strong

I was born and raised in Dorchester, Massachusetts, which is a part of the great City of Boston. Boston is the mecca of champions and home to some of the most historical events of the country. Yet Boston is still considered the little sister to New York City. Growing up, we were always in their shadow. It's true that New York City has a population of over 8 million, ten times the size of Boston. However, Boston has better colleges, hospitals and professional sports teams. Boston has a better quality of life, more space and fewer crowds. Still, for some reason (arrogance, perhaps) they think they are better than us. Maybe Frank Sinatra, "'Ol Blue Eyes", convinced them of their own greatness when he sang of New York, *"If you can make it there, you can make it anywhere."*

Well, I'm Boston Strong, and that's not just a saying. It's a state of mind. I'm also Boston smart, not to be confused with street smart because it is much more than that. Where I come from you have to have tough skin, a strong heart and a willingness to do what it takes to get the job done. The art of taking what you have and making the best of it is a way of life and one of the most valuable lessons I learned from my mother growing up. Through her words and actions I was able to learn the value of a dollar and the necessity and rewards of hard work. During my childhood, we had chores and responsibilities in our home, none of which resulted in an allowance. We didn't get rewards for everything we did. Today kids want to get paid for everything they do. But my mother's philosophy was that this was our home and, therefore, it was our responsibility to keep it clean. She believed in that old saying, *"Cleanliness is next to Godliness."* She provided three meals a day, a roof over our heads and a place to sleep. You were on your own after that.

Consequently, for me to have money, I had to go out and earn it. A lot of times that meant working some labor-intensive, menial jobs. I sucked it up and did it because I wanted my own money and I wasn't afraid of hard work. You wouldn't catch some of my friends doing the work I did because the pay I received wasn't enough for them, plus they were not willing to work the menial jobs. Even jobs at places like McDonald's and Burger King were considered beneath some of them. Back then, my uncle was a manager at one of the premier ice cream restaurants in the state, Friendly's, and he was paid pretty well. But a lot of people wanted fast money and those types of jobs were thought of as lame. It was hard to imagine how a decent-paying, legal job could be considered beneath a kid who was barely living above the poverty line. Right now, I suspect a few million people out of work would love to have one of those jobs.

When the rubber meets the road and you have no way of putting food on the table, you will do pretty much anything. As a result, some of my acquaintances, who took shortcuts and made bad choices, got caught up in the criminal justice system. Some even got involved in violent street crimes and paid the ultimate price with their lives. An old saying warns that "street life" lands you in one of two places: jail or the grave.

People often look for shortcuts to riches. Most shortcuts lead to adverse consequences in the end, yet people are still willing to try them hoping they will hit the jackpot. Example: the scam e-mails from a "Nigerian prince" who is being cheated by his government and wants you to open an account so he can transfer $100 million out of his country. The catch is that you need to put $10,000 of your own money into the account. Then he will transfer the money to you and promises you will get $5 million for your assistance. Sounds ridiculously farfetched, right? I know it does. But desperate people looking for quick financial success have been falling for that scam for years.

The biggest deception perpetrated against the uneducated public is the illusion that you can get something for nothing or that you can get a lot for a little. Believe me, there is no easy system for becoming wealthy. If there were then everybody would be rich. People have taken their

MOTIVATED AND BOSTON STRONG

chances in trying to get rich quickly through multi-level marketing companies like Amway, Primerica and Herbalife. Some people have used other, less known methods. Pretty much anything you can think of people have already tried in their pursuit of riches. However, all the get-rich-quick schemes will only leave you mad, sad and broke in the end. Yet people are willing to take a chance at making millions. Get-rich-quick gimmicks and pyramid schemes are nothing more than fool's gold. Just accept the fact that there is no easy road on your marathon to becoming a financially successful person.

Conversely, with sound practice, patience and consistency you will reach your goal. Remember, you are in a 30-plus-year marathon as opposed to a sprint. If you try to sprint your way to financial success, you will run out of gas. The journey is like running the Boston Marathon. There are flat surfaces, rocky roads and places that are meant to get you to quit, like "Heartbreak Hill." But when you prepare properly, pace yourself and do the things that work, you'll be able to finish strong. Likewise, when the tough times come, and they will, you'll be able to weather the storm.

As a teenager, I would get up at 6 a.m. on the weekends, while most of my friends were sleeping, and ride my bike or take the public bus to the local Stop & Shop supermarket. There, I worked the parking lot. Working the parking lot entailed approaching the store's customers and offering to take their bundles to their cars and packing them. I had to have thick skin because a lot of people would say no, and not necessarily in a nice way. A couple of times people swore at me or told me to "Get lost". But I didn't take it personally. I had a financial goal for the day, so I just went on to the next customer. I could get rejected twenty times, but inevitably somebody would say yes. Usually it was an older lady, who probably respected my honest hustle. After that first "Yes", things tended to pick up. It appeared that these people, seeing others allow me to take their shopping bags, felt safe with me carrying theirs. When I worked really hard I earned about $15 or $20 on a Saturday. It typically took the whole day, so that meant I gave up the Saturday morning cartoons as well as hanging out with my friends, but it was well worth the sacrifice. Back then, that was good money for a teenager.

You could do a lot with it if you spent it wisely. I was resilient and typically did well. I was making sales and didn't even realize it. I guess this was what led me to become a successful consumer foods salesman.

Besides selling my services at the supermarket, I would do all kinds of odd jobs, anything you could imagine. I would do basement cleanup, and I'm talking about some of the darkest, nastiest, rodent-filled basements that you didn't even want to walk through, never mind spending three or four hours on a Saturday trying to clean. Other times I chopped wood. That wasn't easy at all. Imagine this inner-city kid wielding an ax and splitting firewood. It was a sight to be seen. It's a wonder I never cut myself, but there were definitely some close calls. Nothing was simple. Even the times I cut grass were hard, since I had to chop down the weeds first (the electric weed whacker had yet to be invented). Then, when the weeds were all cut and bagged, I still had to cut the grass with a manual lawn mower. Real, tough manual labor creates character and builds a strong work ethic when you are young.

There really weren't any difficult manual jobs I wouldn't do, if the price was right. I wasn't afraid of hard work, knowing that at the end of the job I would be fairly compensated. Those work experiences put calluses on my hands and taught me more than anything about the necessity of a good education because I knew I didn't want to work with my hands for a career. For that time, I worked whatever job was available. Some people spend half their lives trying to impress others. I never understood why people care about what others think of them. Trust me, you will never reach your personal or financial goals if you are consumed with what others think of you. I live to impress no one. I live to serve humanity, provide for my family, and leave an inheritance for my children and my children's children.

As a result, any practices and strategies that allow me to save, invest and profit I take full advantage of, regardless of how silly or miserly it may appear to others. Don't be afraid or embarrassed to implement the practices I share with you throughout the pages of this book. The strategies are not always appealing, but that doesn't matter because they work. You are building a financial foundation one dollar at a time. The Bible says, *"Little becomes much when you put it in the Master's hands."* Translated into Terrance's terms, *"Every time you save a dollar, you are one step closer to your goal."* While you are sacrificing, keep a positive attitude. Embrace the process. Make a sport out of it. Challenge yourself to find deals and bargains. The more you find, the stronger your finances become. You are creating a vaccine that will combat the sickness of being broke. *Do not* fear or fall victim to the spendthrift peer pressure or negative talkers. They create a toxic environment that attempts to stifle creativity, high aspirations and financial success. The old saying, *"Misery loves company"* is alive today. And I'll go a step further and say, *"Being broke loves company too."* Having a companion with whom to commiserate about reasons for lack of success helps deflect the burden elsewhere. It provides false comfort for the unfulfilled, overextended and those with a dearth of financial discipline. They hate their financial condition. Society is full of these types of people. Some of them are in our families.

And strangely, they look down on you for your good stewardship.

Trust me when I say this: financial success is one of the great equalizers. It's not about the love of money. It's about the value you gain through sound practices and sacrifices. For years, my family members and some friends used to mock me for my frugalness. They thought my practices were a bit excessive. Many of them would tease me about my supposed cheapness. "Cheap" was their word, not mine. I didn't consider myself to be a cheap person, and I was always willing to help others. Regardless, as the butt of many jokes, I was never offended or took them to heart. No one else was going to tell me how to spend my money. I worked hard for my money, and I had different plans than most of them did. I dreamed of attaining a financial status that would allow me to never experience financial want. It wasn't that I didn't like finer things; the fact was I didn't value them as many others did. I wasn't willing to spend hundreds of dollars on designer clothes and expensive sneakers. I saw so many people waste what I considered hard-earned money on expensive things and they had nothing to show for it.

Many of them didn't see the irony of having designer jeans and fancy leather jackets with an empty wallet. I liked some of the designer clothes too. And sometimes I got designer clothes, but I never paid full price for them and that was the fun part. We had a bargain department store in downtown Boston called Filene's Basement, which sold all the designer products. I would go down there and rummage through the piles of clothes and wrestle with the other shoppers for the best deals. Nine times out of ten, I would find the same designer clothes for a portion of the money the big spenders paid. To me, the joy was in seeing how much I could save or keep in my pocket as opposed to spending it.

Too many times I saw low-income people competing with one another to obtain the most expensive cars and things. I had no desire to *"keep up with the Joneses."* When I was a teenager, a couple down the street from me had his and hers luxury cars with their names inscribed on the vanity license plates. It seemed like every year they would upgrade their vehicles. They were the envy of the neighborhood because they appeared to be swimming in money. But that's all it was, an appearance. If I could go back in time as a seasoned investor, I would give them some good advice. All the money they spent on new cars could have been invested in a house or another appreciating asset (most new cars depreciate in value the day you drive it off the lot). That one change could have empowered them financially and opened up opportunities for them to do more with their money. I say this not to disparage them, because they were not an anomaly. There are thousands of stories similar to this one in every city throughout the United States, and that's a major problem. Poor money management has kept a lot of people broke.

I started making good choices when I was young, probably by age 10. Now I want to help young people, especially those who grew up like me, understand the value of taking advantage of available resources as well as making the necessary sacrifices that will help them gain financial success. Wasteful and irresponsible spending will set some individuals back behind the eight ball so far that they may never experience financial stability. It's that simple. They must take control of their destiny, set financial goals and implement a financial blueprint.

Life is full of wins and losses. A good blueprint will help you experience more wins than losses. The collection of experiences will help shape the person you are. Sometimes a loss can create a paradigm shift in your life and help position you for success. One loss I experienced that helped shape me occurred during my sophomore year in high school, and I'm certain it kept me on the straight and narrow. It was my own version of *Scared Straight.* I'll share that story in the pages ahead.

6

PERSONAL ACCOUNTABILITY

Experts say you start developing character as a child as soon as you can walk and talk. As with anything, some people grasp it faster than others. We truly can only test character when we have the opportunity to reveal it. The famous UCLA basketball coach, John Wooden, said, *"The true test of a man's character is what he does when no one is watching."* Although people may make mistakes or intentionally do things they know are dishonest, they usually feel bad about what they have done and suffer from what we regard as a guilty conscience. Not everyone feels remorse about past mistakes. When one feels no remorse, it says something about his character.

I'm proud to have been able to own up to my transgressions and live my life with a clear conscience. Growing up, I was usually a pretty decent kid. I made my share of mistakes and played my share of childish games. However, when I became a man I put away childish things and steadily worked on improving myself. An honest and realistic assessment of yourself will help you be the best you can be in your personal and professional relationships. It's critical when you are dealing with your finances. I know my strengths and the areas where I need growth. I consider myself to be a trustworthy person. I have integrity and am known as a man of my word, both in my spiritual life and my personal life. If I say I'm going to do something, unless there are serious, extenuating circumstances, I am going to do what I say. Being trustworthy is important to me, especially in business and finance. When I was a kid in the neighborhood we would sometimes solidify things by saying, *"My word is bond."* That meant something. It meant you had to be true to your word and do what you said you were going to do.

Most things in life are a process, and financial planning and obtaining financial success are not excluded. Earlier I mentioned the dangers of taking shortcuts when striving to accumulate wealth. Shortcuts are only beneficial when you are traveling down the highway. Other shortcuts in life can lead to pain, bankruptcy and extreme disappointment.

If you were to poll all of my friends and family about me, they would probably say I am a straight-edge, hardworking, honest family man. I am, but those attributes don't make me perfect. Most of my family and friends think I've never done anything wrong, including jaywalking. Let me set the record straight. I'm flawed like everyone else. I have made my share of mistakes and bad choices. I'm no goody-two-shoes by any stretch of the imagination. The biggest thing about my mistakes is that I learned from them and chose not to repeat them.

It's relatively easy to do the right thing when you know people are watching. Most people work extra hard when they know their superiors are around monitoring their work. Some of you are saying, *"Not me, I always work hard."* That might be true, but there are others who don't have that work ethic. Some of us may even goof off when we are away from supervision and monitoring; we tend to let down our hair. Many of us strictly adhere to the speed limit on the highway when we know law enforcement is around. Our foot tends to get a little heavier on the gas pedal when there is no cop in sight, especially when we are in a hurry to get somewhere. Eventually, when we get caught not paying attention or flagrantly breaking the rules, we have to pay the price with a warning or fine, and we chalk it up to experience. Usually, the consequences aren't too painful.

Some lessons in life you have to learn the hard way. One important lesson I learned was the universal business law, *"There is no such thing as a free lunch."* That lesson cost me my first real job at Bailey's Ice Cream Shop. Boston has some of the best ice cream parlors in the country. In high school, I was fortunate to have worked for one of those fine establishments. While my time there was short and I didn't leave on my own terms, it was still a blessing and a character-shaping experience. At the time, it was a great job, and I was really happy to have it though I sabotaged myself. If you have ever been fired, it's a pretty humiliating experience, especially if it's due to your own personal transgression. You have no scapegoat and no one to blame but the man in the mirror. Major events in life present learning opportunities. Nowadays, they call what I went through a teachable moment. In addition to the no-free-lunch lesson, I learned two other lessons that were life-changing. First, and most important, *"Always do the right thing."* Second, in any job or company where you are employed, you have a fiduciary responsibility to treat the company's money like it's your own. I didn't always do that and it cost me a really good job that I liked. I remember that fateful day like it was yesterday.

One day, while working at Bailey's, a friend came into the ice cream shop and ordered a sandwich and some ice cream. I filled his order, gave him his food and walked to the cash register acting as if he had paid. It was a routine hookup we did all the time. I had real bravado to be so liberal with OPM (Other People's Money). Back then, the ice cream shop didn't have any cameras. So when I didn't ring up the order in the cash register, there was no evidence of a transaction, unless someone was watching me. I was absolutely reckless. I must have done this a dozen times or more for different friends. This day, like many others before, I made the same unethical decision not to charge my friend. Unbeknownst to me, a visiting general manager from another location was sitting at a table close to the register, and he witnessed everything. After my friend left the shop, the general manager angrily approached me and asked, "What do you think you're doing?" I had no answer for him; I was caught red-handed, doing something I knew was wrong. He fired me on the spot. I remember feeling humiliated and embarrassed. I also remember selfishly feeling mad that I was the only one that had been fired. Most, if not all, of the workers had been doing the same thing, hooking people up every day. We had an exchange going on, trading free food for discounts on sneakers and posters at a sporting goods store down the street. You could call what I did mismanagement, poor stewardship or just plain stealing. No matter how you look at the situation, I was wrong. It was a tough lesson to learn; nevertheless, I'm grateful that I was only fired and nothing more came of the situation. Yes, it was devastating at the time, but at least I didn't have to go to jail or court and have a criminal record. Also, it didn't prevent me from getting another job. Things could have ended very differently for me. There are people sitting in jail for similar offenses because what I did was considered misdemeanor larceny.

When I think about that experience, I'm still shocked that it happened, considering what I was taught back then. My mother was an honest person who operated with integrity. There were two things she hated: "stealing and lying." Pretty much anything else would get you a pass, but if you broke either one of those rules, there was a good chance you would be punished. In other words, you would "get a beating". She wasn't abusive, but she made sure you remembered what you did. She taught my brothers and me right from wrong and expected us to do right.

Sometimes things happen in our lives to prepare us for future blessings. I'm not a big karma guy, but I do believe things happen for a reason. The Bible says, *"All things work together for the good of those who love the Lord and are called according to His purpose"* (Romans 8:28). Who knew that one day I would be steward over millions of dollars in corporate America? I had no idea what my future had in store for me at the time.

7

Obtain Wealth, Not Debt

The seventeenth century English historian, Thomas Fuller, said, *"Debt is worse than poverty."* The Bible says that debt puts us into financial slavery. King Solomon wrote in the book of Proverbs, *"The borrower is a slave to the lender"* (Proverbs 22:7). Faith is a major part of my life. I credit my spiritual relationship with my Creator for developing me into the man I am today. Throughout this book, from time to time, I quote or reference some key scriptures from the Bible that I feel are important and appropriate to the subject matter and the message I am trying to convey. I want to be clear that I am not attempting to impose my spiritual beliefs upon you. Spirituality is personal, and I embrace the notion that your spiritual journey may be different from mine. My purpose and motivation is to assist you in obtaining financial success. I want you to experience an abundant life, which will allow you to enjoy the fruits of your labor.

It will serve you well to accept the view of Napoleon Hill, who said, *"Great achievement is usually born of great sacrifice and is never the result of selfishness."* As far back as I can remember, all I ever wanted to do was grow up and be successful and wealthy. As a result, I made the practice of sacrificing a part of life from a young age. Now, I don't want to give the impression that I started saving and thinking about my future at age eight. But it was around that age that mentors and family members began planting seeds in my mind. Still, I played with Tonka trucks and G.I. Joes. I played outside games with the neighborhood kids, such as hide-and-go-seek and freeze tag. But even then, I was smart with my money and didn't spend every dime I had on toys and candy.

Today, a good portion of my sacrifices are faith-based. Giving and volunteering my time to the less fortunate is more of a personal decision.

I constantly strive to be a better person through education and sharing my knowledge and strategies. My desire is to help others create alternative solutions in their lives.

African-Americans and other people of color are adversely affected when it comes to finances. There's an old saying in some African-American communities often applied to the broad-stroke disparity of our nation's economy: *"When white folks catch a cold, black folks get pneumonia"* (Sam Fulwood III). Loosely translated, this clichéd quip means a downturn in the economy might pose hardships for some White Americans, but it's deadly for those Black Americans who are already mired at the bottom of the economic ladder. Whether you know it or not, millions of American families are in crisis. For some families, one more bad decision could land them on the streets. That's a reality many people go to sleep thinking about every night. It doesn't matter how much denying and minimizing people do, many face dooming financial outlooks — up the proverbial river without a paddle. Some are careening downhill into a deep black hole of debt that will inevitably result in bankruptcy and financial devastation. A small percentage of people will not be touched. For example, the ultra-rich (or "one-percenters" as they are called) won't be. They are fine and will always be fine. As the saying goes, *"The rich get richer."* The ugly flipside is that the poor also get poorer. Middle-class families continue to lose equity and are transitioning to the working poor. For those who are holding on by a thread, and workers just coming into the workforce, I want to be a resource for you. Many of you are carrying school loans of $100,000 or more. That debt is like shackles weighing down dreams and goals, hindering people from any chance of upward mobility. They will never completely get out from under that weight, unless they practice sound financial principles.

Let's partner to create wealth and practice the right spending habits, so that when hard times hit, we are prepared. A great way to start is to create and maintain a budget. Recently, I read in a financial magazine that eight out of ten Americans are in debt. If those numbers don't scare you then maybe these will: 200 million people don't have a family budget. The one small choice of maintaining a budget will help you remain on point when it comes to your finances. For example, you'll save time because you won't need to start from scratch every pay period trying to figure out how you're going to divide up your income to meet your needs, wants and investments. In addition, by doing so, you'll be more organized with your finances and less likely to overspend.

It's easy to overspend. Imagine you are at a new company, and on Fridays everyone goes to the local pub after work for appetizers and drinks. You end up spending $60 that week you never budgeted for. That could throw your whole plan off. Budgeting will help you toe the spending line, identify areas of your life where you can cut back, and allocate your resources more appropriately. So, instead of going out every Friday with your coworkers at $240 a month, go out once a month, spending only $60. You'll sacrifice some camaraderie, but you won't have that frivolous $2,000 annual expense.

A good budget also helps you pay your bills on time. Failure to stay on top of and manage your household and personal bills sets off a chain reaction like a snowball running downhill. Paying bills is the least enjoyable thing any of us do. It's right up there with going to the dentist, but it's just as important. If you don't pay your bills, your finances get out of whack. Likewise, if you don't take care of your teeth, they fall out. Yeah, that's a little drastic, but you get the idea. Bills have to be paid and paid on time. There is nothing better than having the finances to pay the bills and not being stressed about where the money will come from. If you find yourself in debt, creating a good budget and paying your bills will help you get out of it. The sooner you get out of debt, the better you'll feel. You will see more clearly and plan for the future, never wanting to return to that place; so much that you will feel motivated about spending less and saving more.

According to Bankrate, nearly 6 in 10 Americans don't have $500 in savings. That number is truly breathtaking, considering we have a population of approximately 330 million people. That means more than half the country is simply flying by the seat of their pants with no clear vision. If you bring home $4,000 per month and your bills total $3,000 per month, make a commitment to save at least 25%. After just one

OBTAIN WEALTH, NOT DEBT

year, your savings will total $3,000. That same $3,000 becomes $15,000 in just five years. This is a great way to save for a future down payment on a home.

Making a sacrifice is one of the most mature things you can do because it can be tough. It's not in our nature to want less and willfully go without. The reality is that it's enticing to have a childlike mentality when it comes to making sacrifices and spending money. Children live carefreely; they live day-to-day without a thought for the future. They are more concerned about the newest toy or game and often have no real idea of where money comes from or the real value of it. Now I see why, when I was younger, the older folks would say, *"You kids think money grows on trees."* I challenge you to resist impulsive, carefree spending that can put you in debt. Give up some of the things you really don't need now to make room for options that will empower you in the future.

8

WISE SPENDING

I'm guessing that just about everyone reading this book has heard the saying, *"A fool and his money are soon parted."* It comes from a short poem by the famous English poet, Thomas Tusser, which he penned more than 450 years ago. Although it is not often quoted today, I heard the phrase several times in my youth. Most times it was said in the context of wasteful spending. It was a blunt, though not so politically correct, way an adult told you that you were wasting your money.

Now, the term "fool" is both offensive and derogatory and almost never found in my lexicon. I say this only to stress that my decision to include the famous quote is not for attacking or insulting anyone personally but to shine light on the madness of wasting hard-earned money with irresponsible spending. Blowing money fast, frivolously and senselessly is not some new phenomenon. I've witnessed it all my life. While it's a compulsion for some, others find it therapeutic in a strange sort of way. Others do it out of habit or from a learned behavior that was handed down to them. Just as my mother was a conservative saver, other parents are less-disciplined spenders. That's not said in judgment, but as a factual point of reference because a lot of people overspend and overextend themselves beyond their means.

Sadly, unbridled spending is a key driver of the U.S. economy. It's no wonder that American consumers are constantly bombarded by Madison Avenue and marketing bunkers throughout corporate America urging them to buy, buy, buy. Companies are so crafty and sophisticated in their marketing campaigns that most of the time we are oblivious to the overt and subliminal messages they constantly pepper us with. As a result, every day, people purchase large ticket items like cars and giant-screen televisions and other consumer items which they don't need and usually can't afford. This behavior has become a part of the American way. I want to do my part to help change this paradigm. I strongly believe that, if you are willing to sacrifice and learn financial strategies and discipline, you can be successful and achieve your financial goals.

Many people fail at financial prosperity partly due to a lack of knowledge. You may not be aware, but there is a concerted effort to keep you in debt and constantly working to pay that debt. It's no surprise that a large segment of our population lives paycheck to paycheck. Not only that, more people rely on going in to debt to pay their bills than you can imagine. The total sum of credit card debt in the U.S. is not only staggering, it's backbreaking for many. Now, I'm not telling you there is some grand conspiracy, nor am I implying that the government and banks operate nefariously to keep us bound forever by debt. However, I will say this: our banking system welcomes and encourages debt as a way of keeping money flowing and growing the economy. It's in the banking system's, and therefore the economy's, best interest for you to circulate your dollars over and over. I'll let you make your own conclusions from there.

The point I'm trying to make is that retailers and their slick marketing people, backed by the banking system, keep Americans spending beyond their means. I want to help change this paradigm, by raising your awareness of this trap that is set for the unwary. I strongly believe that, if you are willing to sacrifice and learn financial strategies and discipline, then you can be successful and achieve your financial goals. But you have to first rewire your brain to be constantly asking yourself, "Do I really need to spend my hard-earned money on that item just because Madison Avenue told me I should, and the banks said I could? Happiness doesn't come from consumerism, but it does come from a stable life. And sound financial decisions go a long way toward creating the stable life we all want.

I have a two-fold mission: to help willing people stop the cycle of crazy and reckless spending, and to assist young professionals entering the workforce to start on the right path. Initially, college graduates entering the workforce were my target audience. However, I have seen numerous older adults with uncontrollable spending habits that have damaged their quality of life. I want to help them stop the insanity as well.

Young professionals have the chance to avoid the traps and pitfalls of money mismanagement. If you do things right in the beginning, you are more likely to stay consistent. I read somewhere that consistency creates accountability. Most people don't wake up one day and decide to start spending money they don't have. If you were to research their spending habits, I'm confident you would find that they were consistent in their spending, or should I say overspending. The more money you have, the more opportunities you have to spend frivolously. I have heard a ton of stories about lottery winners who went broke in three or four years after winning, sometimes squandering millions of dollars. There are even television series created about the lottery because the outcomes are so unbelievable.

Notwithstanding, I believe that there is a group of people who want to change their financial disposition. These people want help but don't quite know what it takes to make the change. Some of their hesitation may be due to fear of the level of sacrifice required. Yet they are tired and want off that rollercoaster. The stress that comes with that lifestyle has taken a toll on them, and they just want a calm and predictable life. Some see retirement slowly creeping upon them, and they have no real financial plan past Social Security, which is no guarantee for the next generation. A tremendous concern people have is whether or not they'll have enough money to retire when they're ready. Many economists predict that Social Security could be insolvent by 2030. Those depending on Social Security may be waiting on a payday that never comes. I strongly urge anyone who is a part of that population to create a savings and investment plan; it may be your only saving grace. Things can get a lot worse. Countries and economies can collapse. It has happened throughout history, and a bankrupt government cannot pay you. Have you ever heard the saying *"You can't get blood from a stone?"*

Over the years, I've heard some outrageous stories about people making ill-advised decisions when it comes to spending. Picture a woman working 40-50 hours per week to earn $600, then deciding to spend $400 of her check on a pair of designer shoes. That scenario is more common than you might think. To me, it presents a perfect opportunity to reevaluate priorities. Contrary to popular belief, overextending yourself is not a competitive sport, and the only rewards are usually misery and pain.

There are a couple of extreme examples I want to share, with the hope that you can take something positive away. As I grow older and my opinions evolve, I realize people have different levels of financial discipline. Over and over, some consumers appear to make questionable decisions that have an enormous impact on their wellbeing. With that said, I do realize that everyone's story is different and the situation they may find themselves in is not always within their control.

I read a story about a young lady who worked very hard and put in overtime every week at her job. Yet she appeared to be living above her means. She had all the fancy designer clothes and expensive handbags. She looked as if she had it all going on.

Looks can be deceiving though. Reality set in one week when she forgot to submit her timesheet to the payroll department. All hell broke loose and she became completely unglued on payday when she didn't get a check. As I was reading this story, I couldn't help thinking about the missed opportunity of having an emergency fund for life's rough times. If she'd had an emergency fund, there may not have been pandemonium over a missed paycheck.

As the story continued, she went into the office, frantic and in tears. She cornered her manager and began to angrily share her predicament. She told her manager how she lived paycheck to paycheck, a dilemma that millions of Americans have to live with. She couldn't wait a week to get her check. She only had $11 to her name, and that money had to last until the next payday. She didn't have food in her house; she didn't even have money to take public transportation back and forth to work.

This reminded me of when I was growing up and I didn't have enough money to take the subway to downtown Boston. What an awful predicament to be in. Here was this woman, standing in the office with an outfit on that cost hundreds of dollars, carrying a $2,000 Louis Vuitton bag, and all she had was $11 to her name. It was tempting to judge her, and even call her crazy or irresponsible. However, the reality is that I didn't know what else was going on in her life at the time, and quite frankly, it wasn't my business. For all I knew, the Louis Vuitton bag she was carrying could have been a gift, not a frivolous purchase. I am not too old to remember the days when our family had to wait for payday to come in order to pay our bills. There was nothing like the feeling of relief knowing my paycheck was deposited into my bank account and bills could be paid. Rather than passing judgment, I would like to use this story as motivation to change your approach to spending. I can't imagine too many things much worse than needing to pay the rent or mortgage, buy groceries and other expenses, yet be completely broke. I feel for those who have that as their reality, especially when it's due to circumstances beyond their control, such as job loss, illness, or insurmountable medical bills. The teaching moment comes when that situation is created because of needless spending and no preparation.

I heard another story about a guy who seemed to be living above his means. Let's call him William to protect his identity. William had a decent job with average credit, but he wasn't nearly as wealthy or well off as he pretended to be around his relatives and peers. Who knows if it was pride, arrogance or low self-esteem, but William did things and made decisions that were inconsistent with his salary and financial situation. "How would anyone know?", you might ask. You don't have to be a busybody to know that a $75,000 salary only goes so far. But William, like so many others, wanted to live a Dom Perignon lifestyle on a Budweiser salary, and eventually those decisions caught up with him. William and his family would vacation a couple of times a year. They would go out to dinner once a week. Every day, William bought coffee and lunch from one of the many restaurants downtown near his office complex. One of the first lessons you learn in high school is the concept of credit versus debit. If you put out more than you take in, you're in big trouble. You are headed down the road to bankruptcy.

Last summer, William took his family on a beautiful, all-inclusive, seven-day trip to the gorgeous country of Jamaica. Between airfares, the hotel room and all the ancillary expenses that come with it, a trip like that for a family of five could cost you upwards of $8,000; and that estimate is on the conservative side, given the entirety of their trip. While on the trip, William and his wife posted all the wonderful details on Facebook and Instagram. They went on a scuba diving excursion. They attended a world-class seafood buffet and went jet skiing. Their trip looked fabulous! In the eyes of everyone who knew the family and saw the trip on social media, everything *was* fabulous. People had no clue what was on the other side of that spectacular vacation.

Sometimes social media can be deceiving. Many people on social media are perpetrating a fraud, creating a life they wish they had, as opposed to the life they really live. William was one of those people. Instead of living his truth, he was living a very expensive and destructive lie. His electric, cable, water and gas bills, car insurance, and most importantly, his mortgage all went on hold for this trip. When he got home, he had late bills sitting in his mailbox, and he didn't have the money to pay them. To make matters worse, he was forced to take a year's worth of loose change from his daughter's change jar to the supermarket's coin machine in order to buy the weekly groceries for his family. Talk about "from the sublime to the ridiculous." Just a week ago, William and his family were on social media, sitting on the beautiful white sandy beaches of Montego Bay, drinking rum punches, staring into the beautiful turquoise water, eating king crab legs, colossal shrimp and giant lobster tails. He had to be thinking what a difference a week made, as he looked down at his plate of spaghetti, with very little meat sauce, and no-name soda.

William's story was painful to hear. Financial irresponsibility is rampant and the disease of excessive debt is stressful, financially crippling and depressing. I'm not a psychologist and won't pretend to know what William's motives were for his choices. Some people spend to impress, some spend to fit in; the list goes on and on. I have compassion for him and others who have similar spending habits. For those of you who are on the verge of getting out of control with spending, I challenge you to evaluate your buying habits and identify opportunities to make some changes. I believe a good place to start is to adopt a new mentality, one that minimizes needless spending and maximizes wiser, more rewarding decisions.

Every day people make decisions that hurt their financial stability. Every week on payday, countless people make poor choices, like the ones in the stories I just shared. In the past, when I used to hear of such things, I would chime in and ask, "Why are you wasting money on that item?" Every now and then people got offended, and some even indignant, telling me they could spend their money on whatever they wanted because they earned it. Or they might say, "*I don't tell you how to spend your* money." Then they would critique my spending habits. My intention was never to offend but rather to bring them into the knowledge and power of wise spending. In my opinion, it's foolish to take the position that just because you like something, and you can afford to purchase it at the moment, it's a good decision to buy it. It's a childish way of looking at things. There are a lot of people who live an instant-gratification life; who throw caution to the wind for tomorrow to satisfy the flesh today. But I also feel spending just because you can afford to is a dangerously unwise disposition. I guess that's part of the reason some people view me as being cheap or frugal. Ironically, some of those same name-callers learned the hard way when they overextended themselves and wound up in financial trouble. Some of them recognized the shrewdness of my perceived cheapness. They learned that making sound financial choices doesn't automatically equate to being cheap.

I share my strategies with people to help them live financially sound. There are no real secrets to my success. Much of my success has come from sacrifice and sound decision-making. As for the two individuals in the examples I shared, one could wonder how different their scenarios would have been had they used some of the strategies I've been talking about. What if the young lady with the sharp outfit had created a budget? What if William paid his overdue bills on time, instead of splurging on a 7-day vacation? As I said, I don't know their whole stories and there are no guarantees, but I would bet things would be different.

In the end, we all deserve to have nice things or treat ourselves to a much-needed vacation after a stressful year of work. That's not the issue.

The question is, "Does your trip fit your budget?" Think about it. What's the point of going on an extravagant vacation, only to come home to a mountain of debt? Vacations are for rest and relaxation. In addition, they contribute to healthy living, which studies have shown make you more productive in your career. But they should never come at the cost of excessive debt, something we can definitely live without.

Personally, I love to travel and stay in nice resorts. Because of several years of financial discipline, I have the flexibility to go on worry-free vacations. That's the benefit of creating a budget and sticking to it.

9

EQUITY AND WEALTH

Marriage is a beautiful thing. My marriage to Deloris elevated and transformed me. It was one of the greatest and proudest moments of my life. It may sound corny, but out of all the beautiful flowers in the garden, God picked out the most special one and gave her to me. The moment I laid eyes on Deloris on Bentley College's campus, I knew that I was looking at the future Mrs. Bacchus. Call it love at first sight or call it what you want, but I knew we were destined to be together. I can attest to the unmerited favor I have received throughout my adult life because of my relationship with this woman.

It's wonderful to dream, but there is no greater satisfaction than having the ability to turn your dreams into reality. Having a wonderful partner helps make the journey even more fulfilling. Tragedies and the cares of life force dreams to go dormant and unfulfilled. I'm proud to have a partner who believes in perseverance and overcoming, just as I do. I agree with the new, widely used saying, *"Happy wife, happy life."* I also agree with the phrase, *"Teamwork makes the dream work, but teammates make the team work"* (Lance Loya). While both philosophies are definitely true, I coined my own phrase, *"Happy teams achieves the dreams."* Deloris and I worked diligently, sacrificed and exercised patience to reach our goals. Failure was not an option. Someone might say failure is not a choice. Sometimes it is. Sometimes it's the result of a lack of discipline, enthusiasm and dedication. I believe the success of our marriage and the ability to achieve our goals wouldn't have occurred had we not worked harmoniously. It wasn't easy, but we had faith. The tests of our faith caused us to develop the patience to wait on God and the persistence to cultivate the skills necessary to live out our dream.

We have been truly blessed in so many areas of our lives. We worked hard for our blessings, earning everything that we have. Nothing was given to us. And I don't make that declaration out of pride. We had to position ourselves to succeed, which meant living a life of integrity, moving by God's Spirit and hearing His word. Waiting to hear His voice is tough to do because we live in an instant gratification society that wants everything right in the moment. I am not immune to those feelings. But you have to be mature enough to see the big picture and be willing to wait patiently for your time to come. When it does come, you have to seize the moment.

Deloris and I have stood the test of time, and our bond has only gotten stronger over our 27-plus years of marriage. Our financial prosperity is the result of a concerted effort to stringently live within our means. That means we invest first and spend what's left. Because we are with one accord, we have been able to successfully follow our plan. This practice has proven beneficial and dates back to our first days as newlyweds living on a modest income.

When Deloris and I graduated from Bentley College, we talked about things we wanted to accomplish. Starting out, we were ambitious and wanted the world. We were ready to go after our goals and live The American Dream. We studied, worked throughout college and aimed to do all the right things with our money. We felt that effort was critical to achieving our goals. There are an alarming number of college graduates who come out of school saddled with debt and bad credit. We didn't want to get stuck in that trap, so we started out on good footing and began to build up our credit from day one. As we entered the workforce, we were disciplined with our spending. Our first apartment was nice and cozy, but we didn't plan on being there long. We wanted a house of our own with the white picket fence in the suburbs. The 2.5 kids would come later, after we traveled and lived more. Paying rent every month with no equity or anything to show for our money got old really fast. We would never get ahead if we continued in that rut. We had to get our own home and start accumulating equity and wealth.

Owning real estate, more specifically owning a home, is one of the easiest ways for families to begin to create wealth. I challenge every graduate to make purchasing a home one of your top priorities. Buying a car may be a necessity, but

I would not recommend purchasing a new one. Your time for purchasing a new car will come. Focus on the purchase that will provide the greater return on your investment.

Just starting out, it's not always easy to purchase a home, but there is an abundance of resources available if you are willing to do the research. You will soon come to see that any major purchase in your life requires you to do the homework. You have to count up the cost before making life decisions. Deloris and I didn't have a whole lot of knowledge about the process of homeownership, so we attended a few seminars. The seminars opened our eyes to all the benefits and furthered our resolve. We quickly learned why purchasing a home is better than renting. One of the biggest advantages was the ability to deduct mortgage interest on your taxes. We capitalized on that in a major way, using money to finance some of our early family vacations. Conversely, our housing deduction for rent was capped and didn't benefit us at all. Also, as home values increase, the equity would belong to us versus belonging to a landlord. Accumulating equity was the key.

Being new to the professional workforce, we didn't have much in the form of a down payment. We had to work hard to come up with the 10% minimum down payment. Our low down payment meant we had to sacrifice the more expensive locations we desired, Natick and Framingham. That didn't stop us because we knew that home-ownership was the goal, even if it meant we had to give up some things like location and size. We were blessed to purchase our home in Franklin, Massachusetts, which would become the fastest growing town in the state. Because of our sacrifice, we were fortunate to see a major return on our small investment when we sold our home seven years later. Although you may not see it at the time, God always has a purpose and a plan for your life. And if you listen to His still, small voice, He will position you exactly where you are supposed to be.

As I stated, I relish the financial responsibility. I wake up looking for ways to save and invest, accumulate wealth and eliminate debt. I remember the days when I would purchase the annual Entertainment Book for around $20. This small investment included over fifty "Buy One Get One" restaurant coupons, hotel discounts, and many other savings. The first time we used one of the coupons at dinner, we saved enough to cover the cost of the book. I have never felt any shame in using coupons because the money saved turned into money I invested. I even tried helping out family and friends by purchasing them an Entertainment Book as a gift. Thinking back, I was actually sharing tips and didn't realize it.

My family has a financial playbook filled with rules for our finances. We created our own personal rules and incorporated some from Warren Buffet, Dave Ramsey and other leaders in the financial arena. Our biggest rule is that, aside from a mortgage, we don't believe in owing anyone or anything. Debt-free living has to always be at the forefront of your mind, whenever spending is involved. When I think back to some of the various nicknames I was given over the years from family and friends, like cheapskate, miser, and tightwad, I realized that they missed the most appropriate one. The one they really should have been calling me is "Debt-Free Tee." I like the sound of that one, and it's the most accurate and appropriate.

I'm a stickler for paying household bills on time. In those very few instances when I didn't pay on time, it pained me. Why would I want to pay a penalty because I wasn't disciplined enough to look at due dates? That was totally irresponsible and there was no excuse for it. That was money down the drain that I could never get back. If you are not focused, you can easily push bills aside and defer payments. In the end, you have to pay them, and you will end up paying more due to the late fees. Don't waste money!

Before I ever heard of the brilliant business wizard, Warren Buffet, I shared his same disposition when it came to rules about my money. His motto was:

- **Rule #1**: Never lose money.
- **Rule #2**: Never break Rule #1.

Also, frequently making late payments can wreck your credit score. Credit scores are key to financial stability. Your score is easy to damage and difficult to repair. Once damaged, it takes a long time to fix. The last thing you want is to be in the process of trying to purchase a home and find out your credit is bad.

When it comes to credit cards, use them with discipline and use them as infrequently as possible. When you do use them, have a purpose and a plan. For example, my wife and I use one credit card to pay all of our bills each month. However, we don't charge anything we are not in a position to pay off at the end of the month. Why use a credit card at all? First, it helps you build credit. Second, you can earn cash back (amounts vary by company). I don't know about you, but I'd prefer to earn money from the credit card companies, rather than pay them interest. When you attend one of my workshops, I will walk you through my process, step-by-step. You too will learn how to earn money by paying your bills.

10

RESPONSIBILITY TO GIVE BACK

My wife and I decided very early in our marriage to strive to put God first in every area of our lives. A big part of our belief system is to give back to those in need. Giving isn't always about money; we give of our time and talents as well. We volunteer at church and in the community we reside in. Additionally, each year we set aside money to make donations to worthy causes. In past years, we have given to the Susan G. Komen Foundation, United Way, Crohn's & Colitis Foundation, and our *alma mater*, Bentley University. There is an old saying, *"Put your money where your mouth is."* We stand on giving back because we believe that God has blessed us to be a blessing to others.

One way we give back is through tithing. Our commitment to tithing has never been up for debate. There are hundreds of scriptures in the Bible that deal with money, money management and the necessity of it. Ecclesiastes 10:19 says, *"Money answers all things."* That's a powerful scripture that makes it clear that money is needed but must be managed appropriately. I believe that if you are blessed to have money, then you need to understand how to manage it. There is no better manager and teacher of financial responsibility than God. The Bible says in 1 Corinthians 10:26, *"For the earth is the Lord's, and everything in it."* That means everything in this world belongs to God, including the money I make. He is the One who allows me to prosper and gain wealth. All I'm required to do is be a good steward over what He gives me, and part of being a good steward involves tithing.

Tithing is something a lot of people struggle with. Some struggle because they just don't see the value in giving ten percent of their income to a church or ministry. It's a sacrifice. As for me and my house, we choose to honor the Lord with our first fruits because that first ten percent of our income belongs to Him. I read a quote from Lailah Gifty Akita that said, *"Tithing is an open door to wealth."* I couldn't agree more.

I believe that tithing is one of the best investments you can make. For example, Deloris and I learned this firsthand when we had our kids. No one could prepare us for parenthood. When Jasmine, our first daughter, was born, we were faced with the tough decision of whether Deloris should become a stay-at-home mom. Among other things, daycare issues were creating stress. Ultimately, we decided that it was the best thing to do. Truth be told, I was concerned about how I was going to be able to pay a mortgage and support a family of three on one salary. However, Deloris and I also believed that if we paid our tithes, God would meet our needs. We also made additional sacrifices, like eating in more and renting movies instead of going to the theater. The word of God lets us know that our *"God shall supply all of your needs according to His Riches in Glory"* *(Philippians 4:19).* Also, I read in the Bible that when I brought my tithes into the storehouse or the church, He would open up the windows of heaven and pour out blessings that there would not be room enough for me to receive them. And, He did just that. Tithing brought financial blessings to our family. Shortly after the birth of our second daughter, Janae, I was offered a promotion and asked to relocate to Cincinnati, Ohio. Because my company covered 100% of the relocation costs, we were able to use the equity that built up in our first home in Franklin, MA to purchase a house in the fastest growing city in the Cincinnati area. We were able to choose one of the top school districts in all of Ohio. Aside from the benefit of setting our kids up to receive a great education, we were strategically thinking about our investment. Typically, the better the school district the more home values appreciate. We discovered that to be true each time we relocated for work and purchased a new home.

I never imagined that some of the most successful business and entertainment professionals credit the practice of tithing to a large portion of their financial success. John D. Rockefeller, a tither, whom many consider to be the richest man of all-time, was also one of the biggest philanthropists. John Heinz, the great businessman and ketchup mogul, was a man of faith, much like myself. He believed in the concept of tithing and giving to the less fortunate. William Colgate, whose toothpaste and soap millions of Americans use every day, was a religious man who believed in the power of God. He believed God gave him the power to get wealth and prosper. He started out tithing and eventually worked his way up to giving 30 percent of his income. History tells us that the more money he earned the more he gave back. LL Cool J, The GOAT (Greatest "Rapper" of All Time) and mega television star, credits a major portion of his success and longevity to his commitment to tithing. He has been rapping and acting for more than three decades. Those are just a few of the names that come to mind. But the list goes on and on, and I can add my name to that list.

I know what tithing has done for Deloris and me and our financial success. Giving has opened doors in our lives and allowed us to help others in need. From time to time, family and friends have hit financial hard times and needed some assistance. In those situations, Deloris and I sit down and see how we can help. We do this out of the kindness of our hearts, with no strings attached. We don't believe in conditional giving or even giving only to people we know will have the capacity to pay us back. We do it for the joy and satisfaction we get from knowing that we can make a difference when someone is in need.

You may not believe in the concept of tithing, but please understand that giving is important and critical to your financial success. Many of the world's wealthiest people continue to be some of the biggest givers. Take Oprah Winfrey for example. She is one of wealthiest African-American women in the world. In 2007, she donated $40 million to build a 22-acre leadership academy for girls in South Africa. That's quite a donation. She is not alone. In 2017, Robert F. Smith surprised the entire graduating class at Morehouse College when he announced that he would pay off their student loans which was estimated up to $40 million. What an outstanding way to give back and help reduce the burden of student loans for so many people. Finally, the LeBron James Family Foundation helped build the I Promise School in Akron, OH to help at-risk kids, by giving them the opportunity to thrive despite difficult life situations. Education is near and dear to my heart, which is why I choose to highlight these three stories.

Giving back has to be part of a successful financial plan. But I am not naive to realize that not every person or company makes charitable donations out of the kindness of their heart. Some make donations to help themselves or their business. After all, many charitable donations help reduce your taxable income. You may have heard about companies and/or individuals that have paid little to no taxes. They do so because they found creative, yet legal ways to reduce their taxable income. Simply put, they maximize their dollar, while also giving back.

11

EMPHASIS ON SOCIAL MEDIA

D
on't let social media drive you into financial bondage. All that glitters isn't gold, and all that is posted is not real. I don't know how many times I have heard someone say that social media is the devil. Social media is a great tool if used for the purpose for which it was created. The Facebook platform was designed to allow family and friends to connect and share stories online. Facebook allows me to catch up and communicate with many of my friends all around the country. From high school to college and throughout my professional career, I have met remarkable people with whom I like to stay connected, and Facebook allows me to do that. In fact, through Facebook, I contacted Coach Croft and asked him to write the foreword

for this book. I use the LinkedIn platform to manage my professional connections. My overall social media experience, except for a few irrational incidents, has been very positive. Occasionally, some of my Facebook friends have very different goals, values and lifestyles than mine. In those instances, I choose not to share and converse with them. There are no hard feelings; we are just moving in different directions.

Also, what I have found is that people are not always who they claim to be online. Although social media users attempt it every day, you cannot create your own reality. Still, some jump online and create fake or exaggerated identities. They create their own reality, or the life they desire to live. Others have multiple online personalities. I can't count the number of times I've seen individuals make religious or inspirational posts speaking about the power of God, only to see them two hours later posting vulgar language and cursing someone out.

Earlier, we talked about the concept of keeping up with the Joneses. It's never been more prevalent than online. In fact, it has been taken to another level. Lifestyle competition is out of control. Whether it is in weddings, vacations, or something as simple as dinners, people post the most trivial things, constantly trying to outdo one another for likes and shares.

I am pretty conservative with my social media posts. I don't believe everything that happens in my life has to be shared with the world. Throughout this book, I have provided examples of people who have gone crazy spending and have absolutely nothing to show for it but a pile of debt. Don't get caught in the craziness.

The other drawback to this posting of excessive consumerism is that corporations use your posts to manipulate and control your spending, especially in the black community. For example, are you aware that major companies track how you spend your money? They purchase a lot of data many of you provide for free on social media in order to market to you. Many of us are getting exploited and don't even realize it. Take the most popular sneaker company (which shall remain nameless) for instance. They know certain communities love "a certain sneaker line named after a famous basketball player," and cannot wait for the next release date. Therefore, they don't have to spend marketing dollars advertising to that community because they have the market all sewn up. This is not the only company that takes advantage of the excessive spending. There are thousands of companies and people whose sole purpose is to separate you from your money. Television commercials, advertisements, holidays and a host of other schemes want every dollar you earn.

Why am I sharing my thoughts about advertising and marketing? I am doing so because I know the marketing and advertising vehicles are effective in getting you to spend your hard-earned money. I encourage you to use the same dollars for investing. Let's change our online paradigm and make the majority of our posts be about obtaining wealth and happiness and not about unbridled spending. Let's be the change needed for financial success!

12

DECISIONS, DECISIONS, DECISIONS

By now, it should be crystal clear to you that your commitment to financial success and doing what it takes is truly one of the most important decisions of your life. However, it's important to realize that sometimes the right path is not always the easiest one to follow. A life of financial struggles and instability brings unnecessary stress and a burden that will negatively affect your quality of life. The longer you live, the more of life's arrows will pierce you. I have done my best to drill into your psyche the importance of good money management. I hope that you have felt my passion come alive on the pages of this book as I push you toward your destiny. William Arthur Ward, the author of "Fountains of Faith," wrote, *"Before you speak, listen. Before you write, think. Before you spend, earn. Before you invest, investigate. Before you criticize, wait. Before you pray, forgive. Before you quit, try."*

My charge to you is, *"Before you retire, save. Before you die, give. Before you overextend, give yourself the gift of financial independence."* I encourage you to choose to walk the path of prosperity and provisions. Make the precise decision and choose the right path. Commit to implementing some of my suggestions and incorporate them into your financial blueprint. Don't be discouraged. Often, the right path is not pretty or exciting.

Decide to succeed. Reject the wrong path that leads to careless spending and living paycheck to paycheck. It's a difficult existence that results in worry and stress about finances, an existence that keeps millions of people up at night. The inability to plan for the future and the reality of never having enough is taxing.

Those of you who have gone to college intending to get the perfect job and make a great salary, your commencement is just the beginning of a lifelong journey. Those of you graduating from a trade school or whatever profession you have chosen, this is the starting line. You haven't won anything yet. You have just earned the right to be in the race. Winning is doing the right thing over and over and over. Winning is what you do with the money you earn. It's how you make the money work for you, as opposed to you working only for the money. It's not easy. In fact, it's difficult but doable if you remain consistent.

Watching my retirement account grow was great, but it really became rewarding once I entered the stock market. I remember the first time I purchased a stock. I chose a company that I was familiar with and whose brand I trusted. After doing some research on the company's performance, I jumped in with a $10,000 investment. Over time, I watched the investment grow over 600 percent. Now, I am not telling you that every stock I've purchased delivered the same results; some grew much slower and others actually declined. But I am telling you that you have to be in the market to make money. If stocks are too risky for you, there are safer investments like mutual funds or IRAs. Although I encourage to do your homework before selecting one or all of these options, let me give you my personal perspective on each.

Purchasing a stock means you are investing in a company and becoming a shareholder. Usually the company's performance is what drives the prices up or down. Stocks are the most rewarding because they tend to perform the best over time. If you are not much of a risk taker, then the stock market may not be for you. Mutual funds, on the other hand, are much less risky. You are actually purchasing a collection of stocks, bonds or other securities. Therefore, if half the companies in the fund are performing poorly and the other half are performing well, you are less likely to lose money. It's also a great way to have ownership in a company whose stock you may not have been able to purchase due to its high share price. Lastly, an IRA (Individual Retirement Account) is a retirement savings account in which income taxes on certain deposits and on all gains are deferred until withdrawals are made. The key word here is "retirement". All three are great options, but educating yourself on each will allow you to make the best choice for your own risk level.

I have been completely transparent with you. I have shared more of my personal life and journey on the pages of this book than I ever have before. I did so because I truly want you to win. All the good, bad, and even embarrassing things are included so you will know I am no different than anyone else. I'm not special. But I am disciplined and laser-focused when it comes to financial management and the money I earn. I want you to be the same way.

There is an African-American proverb that says, *"Each one, teach one."* That's a great and much-needed philosophy. Yet, in our current financial climate, it doesn't go far enough. This may sound grandiose, but I want to help promote 1,000 millionaires: A thousand people who will commit to making the sacrifices and choices that will not only help them live financially sound and stress-free, but also set up a legacy for their families and allow them to be financially empowered. Life is full of ups and downs and highs and lows. Things will come at you out of the blue, unexpectedly and unscheduled. Some of those challenges will knock you to your knees. Money will not be the answer to all things. However, it will help solve many of your problems. Therefore, having a strong financial foundation will help you manage a great deal of those challenges.

13

JUST BE DISCIPLINED

Someone said, *"It's easy to make money, but it's hard to keep it."* It's more appropriate to say, *"It's easy to make money but it's hard to manage and grow it."* My declaration is like Donna Summers' old song, *She Works Hard for the Money.* Not only do I work hard for my money, I work smart for it. As a result, I want to do all that I can to keep as much money as I can. By now, you have heard me say at least a dozen times that sacrifice and smart decisions have to be a way of life. Not to beat a dead horse, but those two choices are probably the most important things you can do to build your finances. There is no getting around the process unless you have generational wealth being handed down to you. Even if that's the case, you can use my strategies to create more wealth. What's better than one million dollars? How about two million dollars?

Besides sacrifice and smart decisions, you must also practice good discipline. Discipline is a seriously undervalued trait that when practiced can alter your life. It helps you maintain a level of consistency across all areas of your life. Moreover, what good is it to sacrifice in one area of your spending only to spend irrationally in another area? For example, some people think it's senseless to pay $5 for a cup of coffee. I agree, but in true transparency, I am not a coffee drinker. Conversely, some of those same people will turn around and spend $50 on a pair of socks or $1,000 on a handbag. To the $5 coffee drinker, those purchases seem absurd. I don't believe either of these examples are wise. Don't think of me as the spending police, here to judge your every purchase. By the time you finish this book, you will hopefully want to save first or at least think twice before you spend. I'll be that proverbial spending angel on your shoulder, challenging you to make wise and prudent choices. CEO of the company DUE, John Rampton says, *"Don't let money run your life, let money help you run your life better.*"

When I was growing up, my elders would say, "*Stop and think before you speak.*" I want you to apply that same energy and, "*Stop and think before you spend.*" Develop a realistic and manageable plan and stick to it. Starting off on the right track will make things easier. A clean, fresh start does wonders and that's largely the reason why the biggest population of my focus is college students and young professionals. The hope is that they have not already developed bad spending habits. In the cases where they have, we can introduce replacement behaviors and alter the outcome. On the other hand, it's hard to tell adults who have been doing the same thing for twenty-five years that they need to stop their bad behavior and do something else, even when you make the advantages crystal clear. Daily, people make conscious choices that negatively affect their quality of life, whether it is in the area of finances, health, or other areas of life.

Our country, as a whole, has financial problems. Some small segments are doing very well and prospering at unprecedented rates. However, for the majority of families, personal and family debt is at an epidemic proportion. Every day, people continue to spend money they don't possess on things they don't need. They are spending future earnings on present, inconsequential stuff. Maybe it's a spending problem or maybe it's a case of just doing what they have always done and what they've seen their family do. I don't have the answer. I do know that some people spend to fill a void. Again, discipline is the answer to many of the problems we face.

A recent online article I read stated that millennials are the most likely cohort to opt out of investing in a company 401(k). I don't know if that's because they want to live for today and not think about the future. Maybe it's because they just don't have anyone explaining why it's important.

On my first day at General Mills, I got the best financial advice I have ever received. A friend of mine, Sherry from Bentley College who had graduated a year before me, worked for the company. Sherry reached out to me and said the best thing I could do was take advantage of the generous retirement plan that the company offered. Sherry told me to contribute the maximum amount of before-tax money that I was allowed into my 401(k) retirement plan. Just like most 24-year old college graduates, the last thing I was thinking about was putting money into a retirement account. The future was way off. We hadn't even reached Y2K yet. In the year 1990, the biggest thing we were worried about was what we were going to face in the year 2000. People's anxiety was highly elevated. The big scare and thought was that all the computers were going to stop and the banking and financial institutions were going to fall into chaos. Some even predicted the end of the world. But I was not as concerned; it didn't stop me from saving and investing. Now that we are in the year 2020, and I'm in my 50s, I'm so glad I heeded Sherry's advice. It started me on the road of disciplined saving and wealth building, and I want to do the same for you.

14

ON YOUR MARK. GET SET. INVEST.

The very best investment you can make is in yourself and your future. Investing in others is important as well, but you must come first. That philosophy is not derived from a selfish perspective but rather from a position of empowerment. You can't give what you don't have. And if you don't have an abundance, you only have enough for yourself. There will always be people who need help, whether it be family, friends or whomever. Nonetheless, strengthen yourself up first, and then you will be able to pull up others. The old saying, *"Don't put the cart before the horse,"* is quite appropriate when it comes to investing and empowering others. For you who are just starting your new career, you have a bright future ahead. The sky's the limit.

With that said, right out of the blocks you have to start doing the right thing. Excuse the track reference, but track was a big part of my youth and has real-life lessons I carry with me today. When I was in high school, in order to give myself the best chance of performing well during the 100-meter sprint (or the 400-meter relay), Coach Croft made me spend a lot of time working on my start, coming out of the blocks. This was a great area to work on because the race was so short.

Much like track, the later you start investing, the harder you have to work to catch up to win the race. Also, you have to lean into investing, much like leaning into the finish line of a sprint. The bottom line is, investments, just like track and field and life, is about preparation and execution. When you jump off that block, you have to put your best foot forward. The last thing you want is a false start. Focus and concentration are essential. *"Money, like emotions, is something you must control to keep your life on the right track"* (Natasha Munson).

I truly believe that anyone reading this book can become financially successful, regardless of your upbringing or career of choice. Not everybody is going to work in the corporate world. Some will become entrepreneurs, while others will work a skilled trade. Whatever you decide, the first thing you must do is sign up for the 401(k) on your job. Just like my friend Sherry told me, the most important thing you can do for yourself and your future is to start investing on day one. Invest the maximum and start letting your money work for you. If you are self-employed or your employer doesn't offer one, then you should establish it on your own.

Some people will never have the discipline to consistently contribute to a personal savings plan. They will always find an excuse or reason not to put money away each pay period. But if you contribute, starting with your initial paycheck, you will never miss the money. You can't miss something you never had, plus when you participate in a company 401(k), you get "free money" in the form of matching funds. Most companies contribute anywhere from 2%-6% of your salary (up to a certain dollar limit). While I was employed at General Mills, they contributed fifty cents on the dollar, up to 6%. So, in good years the company could elect to match another 50%, which would equate to a $1 for $1 match. All you have to do is pay attention to your statements and review your account quarterly. At the end of the day, it's your money and you are responsible for managing it. The 401(k), in some instances, can be a lazy man's way of saving and investing, meaning you don't have to do much. Your money will be on autopilot. But even then you still have to pay attention. The amount of detail that you give to doing your job should also be given to monitoring your future earnings.

Your level of involvement can be limited to once a year at your annual review. However, to reach a significant retirement savings goal of $1 million, you have to co-manage your money with your retirement plan administrators. The investment company will explain the process and investment strategies, and you pick the funds that work the best for you. Some people like aggressive, some like passive, some like bonds and others like growth. Again, it's your money and your choice. Whatever you choose, this is the most consistent way to build future wealth. But you have to stay on top of rule changes and additional benefits that become available. Because at the end of the day, who is going to look out for you the most? You, I hope. Sometimes, one decision can have a dramatic effect on your life. Choosing to invest in a 401(k) will do just that.

15

UNEXPECTED EMERGENCY PREPARATION

One of the most significant and valuable personal characteristics you can develop is being proactive. The great Albert Einstein said, *"Intellectuals solve problems but geniuses prevent them."* I'm not referring to myself as a genius because I am far from one. While I am not an expert, I pride myself in my preparation and planning, especially when it comes to my future. I like being prepared for any situation I may encounter. The practice of proactive planning and decision-making has served me well throughout my professional career and personal life. Whether I'm going in for a job interview, going into a department store to make a major purchase, or simply booking a weekend getaway, I like my decisions to be carefully thought out.

Too many things in life are done reactionary or willy-nilly and often end in indebtedness, disorder, and disappointment. I work responsibly to prevent those things from unnecessarily occurring in my life. Benjamin Franklin said, *"An ounce of prevention is worth a pound of cure."*

Because we planned ahead and started making our financial sacrifices after graduating from college, my wife and I have accumulated a very good retirement fund for our family. If we continue to live the disciplined lifestyle that we chose for the last 30 years, I can confidently declare that we are on track to meet our financial goals. Because of our sacrifices, we will be able to leave a sizable inheritance to our children, which was our goal from the outset. That's quite an accomplishment for us, considering we started with nothing but dreams, aspirations and a willingness to sacrifice to reach our goals.

Now, you may not agree with our desire to leave an inheritance to our children. However, this is my way of helping to close the racial wealth gap that exists in our country. At this point in my life, I'm further compelled to help the next generation coming up behind me. As I stated before, I want to help create an army of millionaires from all walks of life that will change the financial landscape of underserved communities and the larger society. If I can help create 1,000 new millionaires, we can help change the landscape of America and put families in a better position to handle the uncertainties of the future.

An abundance of things will occur in life which we will have little or no control over. This is inevitable, so we all need to be ready. To prepare for those hardships, it's imperative that you develop an emergency fund to access when necessary. The best financial advisors will tell you that you should always have a cash reserve of 6-months' worth of income available to cover reoccurring, monthly expenses, (housing, food, automobile, insurance, utilities, recreation, etc.) for any unexpected emergency. Simple math will tell you that if you earn $6,000 a month, then you should have $36,000 in an emergency fund. More recent studies suggest that 7 months' worth of income is more appropriate in the case of an incident that will prevent you from working or earning an income. I'm not including things like disability insurance in the projections.

The world is unpredictable. Jobs dry up every day. Even the very best jobs can be eliminated at the drop of a hat. I don't care how good your job is or how secure you think your employment is, companies downsize every day. There were a few times during my professional career when it appeared my position might be phased out. My company periodically presented early retirement to people, but never directly to me. I probably would have taken it, had they offered. Those experiences showed me the vulnerability of my professional life and reassured my practice of being prepared.

Oftentimes, things come out of the blue and catch us off guard, but we have to be able to re-group and redouble our efforts. You have to be able to bounce back quickly in today's corporate market. I advise you to view those setbacks as opportunities for comebacks. Every day, major companies relocate in their constant pursuit to improve their bottom line. Some companies are heartless, soulless, unfaithful entities willing to do whatever it takes to increase profits. Many of us think much more highly of ourselves concerning our professions than we should. In the grand scheme of things, we are expendables. One day you are on the train, reading your newspaper without a care in the world, on your way to work downtown. Your beautiful corner office with a stunning view of the city awaits you. You get in, work your butt off, and at the end of the day you get an email telling you that in 30 days the company is moving to Mumbai or Bangladesh and you will be out of a job. Every day, lives get turned upside down. No matter what field you work in, you are not immune. So, be prepared. You can love your company, but remember, no matter how much you love that company it can't love you back. Corporate America is not designed that way. Things like love and loyalty are not a part of the corporate structure. This book wouldn't be authentic if I only told you all of the good without including the bad. That's why you should love what you do and avoid getting caught up in who you are doing it for.

Nothing lasts forever, companies fold up every day. No one ever thought Lehman Brothers would go out of business; a company with several hundred billion dollars in assets under management collapsed like a paper cup in 2007 and declared bankruptcy in 2008. People trekked into work one morning, some who had been there thirty, forty, even fifty years, and the doors were locked, the signs were down, and their jobs were gone. Would you call what happened to all those employees an emergency? I wonder how many of those employees had an emergency fund? It's like the old adage about insurance: it's better to have it and not need it than to need it and not have it.

Okay, I'm going to share another part of my life with you. Growing up, our emergency fund was my mom's paycheck she got every Friday. Any financial emergencies had to wait until Friday, and if it was rent week then they had to wait until the following week. I don't know how we did it, but we did. It was the goodness and mercy of the Lord. Now, you have the capacity to create an emergency fund as soon as you begin working. It's one of the most important things you can do.

Hundreds of emergencies come up in life. One which turns everybody's world upside down is when a death occurs. An alarming number of people are not prepared financially. Some of this goes back to the social media issues, where the same people who lived the lifestyle of the rich and famous never bothered to purchase life insurance. They place loved ones in precarious situations, looking for help to bury family members. Now their big-time social media page is filled with GoFundMe and help requests. I don't say this to be disrespectful or unsympathetic. I just want you, the reader, to be fully prepared for all the financial storms that could come your way. A strong, well-rounded financial foundation will allow you to withstand financial storms. Life insurance should be a mandatory purchase in your life. Keep in mind that even when you have insurance, sometimes things can be delayed and the payment may take a while to come. It will likely be okay if you have an emergency fund built up to sustain you.

Do you know you can borrow from your 401(k) in an extreme emergency? It's considered a hardship withdrawal. Guess who you pay back? You pay yourself back and with zero interest. Please understand, this should be a last resort because you will be penalized if you don't repay the money. Nonetheless, the option is there if absolutely needed.

Right now, as I prepare to release this book, the country faces the biggest threat that I have ever experienced in my lifetime. Who would have thought that in the year 2020 we would be fighting a deadly Coronavirus (COVID-19) that would bring the country to its knees? This pandemic has carried our economy to a screeching halt and dealt the stock market some devastating blows that it hasn't experienced since the Great Depression. The Federal Government is teetering on the verge of declaring martial law, states have issued stay-at-home orders, and thousands of companies and sections of our economy have been shut down.

Millions of people are out of work and have no way to pay their bills, feed their families and keep a roof over their heads. They are at the mercy of the government, and this whole process is driving thousands into severe depression. Furthermore, when the government does provide some sort of financial assistance for those hurting, the amount of money will likely not be adequate to meet their needs.

It's like putting a Band-Aid on a bullet wound, as they say. The whole situation is heart-breaking. I feel for those who are struggling to survive financially and for those who have lost loved ones. When we come out of this, anyone who doesn't have an emergency fund, please establish one. Maintaining an emergency fund account is an *absolute must*. Nothing could have prepared our country for this ordeal. My hope is that those who do have an emergency fund with six months' worth of income are finding it to be a cushion for their families, as they face this devastation. Those of you who have depleted a portion of your emergency fund, make replenishing it a top priority. The end result is that your emergency fund is an investment in your peace of mind when financial trouble comes your way, and it should serve as a teaching moment to all us.

Earlier in this book, I used the phrase, "no shame in my game" when speaking about finding deals. There should also be no shame if you have to ask for help. Maybe the six months' worth of income is not enough, and you need assistance until you can get back on your feet. Don't let shame keep you from asking for help in order to feed your family. Just remember to pay it forward when other people need assistance.

16

Remember Your "Fun" Fund

D on't forget to create a recreation fund or what I refer to as a "fun fund". A recreation fund is of lesser importance in your life, yet still a necessity. We all need downtime – breaks, vacations and hobbies to keep us sane. But just like every other area of our lives, it should be planned and carefully thought out, counting up the cost. No extracurricular activity should put you in a hole, nor should it be financed with debt such as credit cards. In the past, my wife and I used our tax refunds to finance our summer vacations. Whatever we planned had to fit into the family budget. If we wanted to go to Hawaii, we needed to have Hawaii money. We couldn't go to Hawaii on Florida money. But vacations have changed since we started going twenty-seven years ago. There is even a new phenomenon called "*Staycations*," the concept of vacationing at home. It's really not all that new to me because we did that throughout my childhood. It's a little more sophisticated nowadays, but you still need money even for those.

Years ago, credit unions and community banks used to have things like Christmas clubs and vacation clubs. It was a way for people to save money for holidays and getaways. Employees would have their company deduct money from their paychecks, put it in a low or no-interest savings account, and designate it for Christmas or vacations and trips. So, when it was time to take your annual trip to Disney World with the kids, or Jamaica or the Bahamas, you already had the money put aside. It was a novel idea, and it worked for some people. They are still around though not as popular as they used to be. But the concept of finding ways to put money aside is important.

I have two main avenues I want you to consider as practical ways to help you fund your necessary accounts, in addition to traditional savings. The first one I think is relatively easy. Daily, people trek to the local coffee house for their morning cup of joe. Depending on their brand of choice, the waiting lines could be quite long. But, it's a morning ritual for many. Ninety-five percent of the people I have worked with over the past thirty years are coffee drinkers. They need that cup to start their day; some people won't even talk to you until they have their first cup.

The coffee industry makes in excess of $100 billion a year. The cost of a cup of coffee ranges from $1.50 to $6.00, if you are on the high end. Many coffee snobs refuse to drink just an average cup of joe. They want the top of the line. In my opinion, that's why people love their Starbucks, whose sales in 2019 were more than $26 billion. That's a lot of people drinking expensive coffee. I have a relative who loves her White Mocha Latte. She has to have one every morning. It costs her roughly $5.00 a cup. So, she spends $25.00 a week on coffee. That turns out to be roughly $100 a month, which ends up being $1,000 a year if you factor in days off and vacations.

Now, if she takes that same $1,000 and opens an investment account, that Starbucks coffee money, after 30 years could earned her $113,352 (using compounded interest). That is separate and above your 401(k) plan. This is a good time to think about how good that coffee is and if it is really worth the daily expense.

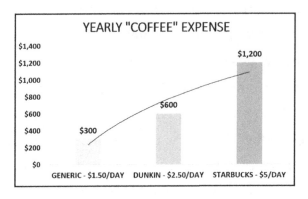

The second avenue to consider has to do with your lunch choices. Getting rid of expensive lunches will help to increase your financial success. Everybody appreciates a good corporate lunch when it is on the company's dime. I've had my share of lavish lunches, but I didn't pay for them. However, when the lunch funds are coming out of your budget, moderation and discretion are advised. I know a lot of young people just starting out who buy lunch every day, and many of those lunches are not cheap.

When I first started out, we only had a limited number of choices for lunch. My choices were fast food options, such as McDonald's, pizza and subs. Chinese food was an option too, but that was about all you had to choose from. Today, you can have anything you want for lunch. It's all available to you with one click. It's a billion-dollar business. All kinds of telephone apps and food delivery services pop up daily, competing for your dollar. They have the ability to bring the restaurant of your choice to your desk. People take advantage of it too. It's not uncommon to see co-workers, who work in all different capacities of the company, eating sushi, lobster rolls, gourmet hamburgers, steak tips and whatever you can think of. Many of them easily spend anywhere from $8.00 to $15.00 a day on lunch alone, and that's on the low end. Imagine if you took that money and invested it instead of eating fancy lunches. Now, I'm not going to be hypocritical; I don't like bag lunches, although I do enjoy my PB&J. When it comes to ordering lunch, I do try to cap myself at $5.00 and I also will save money by picking up vs. paying for delivery. Often, the delivery fee and tip can amount to just as much as the meal. And no, it's not because I don't want to tip the delivery person. I have no problem tipping anyone for good service. There are waiters and waitresses all around my area that love to see me coming in for a meal because they know I don't tip less than 20%. However, if you invested the $100 per month you didn't spend on lunches, after thirty years that same investment account would rise to $226,705 (using compound interest).

Now that's serious money, and it's accumulated by making some relatively easy adjustments in life. I'm willing to bet, and I'm not a gambling man, that if I were to poll 1,000 people who have worked for thirty years, and asked them if they would like to know how to save $226,705, I dare to say 100% of them would say, "Yes".

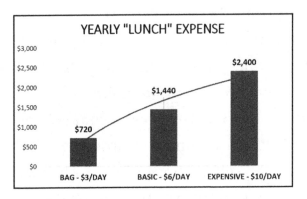

If you choose to make these small choices, you will position yourself for financial success. Just the interest accumulated on that balance alone is about $15,000 annually. You can do a lot with that money if you spend it wisely.

17

No Lotto Tickets

Don't plan your future on luck or chance. There are some age-old, generally proven ways to obtain financial success. Casino gambling and playing the lottery are not two of the ways. They are actually quite the opposite; instead of success they guarantee disappointment and debt. I believe that gambling is a surefire way to waste your hard-earned money. Don't let the bright lights, looks of excitement and the chance at a million dollars trick you into poverty. There is a reason why they are building new casinos all around the country. They wouldn't keep building casinos if they were not successful or at least making profits. Do you know where their profits come from? They come from the thousands of risk-takers that come to their establishments looking to hit it big. Instead, every night those risk-takers drive home dejected and defeated at the hands of one-arm bandits, savvy dealers and sophisticated gambling software that was created to separate them from their money. It's a sucker's bet, a few steps up from the three-card monte game that they used to hustle in the Boston Commons when I was a kid. It's the illusion of the chance at winning.

A lot of people can't get to the casinos, but they can still take a chance at riches locally. Convenience and liquor stores have dedicated space for their patrons to gamble. The lottery is one of the biggest scams and money drains. You can't go anywhere without seeing someone scratching a ticket. The worst is watching countless adults spend money on scratch and lottery tickets, win a few dollars, and turn around and buy more, all before they have left the store. That totally blows me away. It makes absolutely no sense to me. The hundreds of winners don't outweigh the hundreds of millions of losers. The only people truly winning are the casinos and the local governments. The State Lottery is a big moneymaker. In Ohio, my current home state, the profits from the lottery last year exceeded $1 billion. The state made out pretty well; unfortunately, it was on the backs of poor, lower and middle-class people. I don't mean to suggest that they are victims forced to participate in a program. These people walk willingly to the counter and place their money down, taking a chance to win big. Generally, wealthy people don't play the lottery; if they do, it's with disposable income that they can afford to lose. The wise protect the money they earn.

Here are some cold, hard facts and statistics for you to think about before you start wasting your hard-earned money on gambling and lottery tickets. You have about a 1 in 300,000,000 chance of winning Mega Millions' $340 million jackpot that is up for grabs in the next drawing. To put this in perspective, you have a far greater chance of being attacked by a grizzly bear while on vacation at a U.S. National Park than winning that jackpot. That happens every 1 in 2.7 million visits, according to the National Park Service. Despite the long odds, thousands of Americans will buy tickets for a chance to win. According to gallup.com, in 2017 (the most recent year on file) about half the American population played state lotteries with total sales topping $71 billion. According to the U.S. Census Bureau, consumers each spend an average of about $86 a month on lottery tickets, including everything from scratch-off cards that come out of vending machines to entries for the Powerball and Mega Millions competitions. Spending on lotto tickets adds up to about $1,038 each year per consumer according to a recent survey commissioned by Bankrate of over 2,300 U.S. adults. It's worth noting that Bankrate's results are slightly higher than the $70 a month the Bureau of Labor Statistics found the average American spent between the third quarter of 2017 and the second quarter of 2018. If you took that money and invested it in a tax-deferred investment account, after 25 years it would net you somewhere in the neighborhood of $59,000. Even if you just put it under your mattress, you would accumulate $22,500. Either way you look at it, that's good money going to waste, one of my biggest pet peeves.

Now, you may not be a gambler and therefore wouldn't be enticed by the risk-taking. However, we all have some kind of vice or money-wasting behavior that we occasionally indulge in. Think about your vice or area where you waste money, then visualize and calculate what your money could be doing for you.

18

Everything Society Has to Offer

One of Warren Buffet's most cited principles is, *"If you don't find a way to make money while you sleep, you will work till you die."* That may seem extreme to you, but it's a reality that millions of Americans need to come to grips with. Far too many people spend their whole lives on the repetitive hamster wheel of unfulfilled employment (work-payday-spend-repeat). They work until they are 65 or 70 years old, retire and then die, never having fulfilled their dreams or goals. Work is honorable, and everyone who is able should do some kind of work. Our years of working should be toward a goal, and that goal should be for more than paying bills. We should all be living our lives to the fullest, setting goals and going after our dreams, not just existing to service our debt. On a daily basis, people decide to settle and accept whatever the universe and life send their way. That is not why we were created. I have shared my life story with you as a testament of what can be achieved regardless of where you started in your life. You just have to be willing to do the work. It's not easy; if it were then everyone would be doing it. However, it is attainable. I want the readers of this book to dream the way my friends and I dreamed when we were young and the way I dream now. I achieved some of my childhood dreams; one was to become independently wealthy. Too many people live beneath their privilege and put limits on life's expectations. I am challenging you to go after everything society has to offer. A big piece of my philosophy and winning formula is to live beneath or at least within your means. To do that, it takes discipline and determination. However, it will change your life. It worked for my mom, it worked for Warren Buffet, it worked for me, and believe me, if you practice it and remain steadfast, it can work for you too. And a collection of financially sound people can change a community and a generation.

19

You Are Ready For the Challenge

The famous writer Mark Twain said, *"Twenty years from now you will be more disappointed by the things that you didn't do than by the ones you did do."* It's natural and normal to look back on life and have some regrets about decisions made or deferred. Reflection is good. It allows you to maintain a proper perspective, grow emotionally and make better choices. You don't want to think back on the *"would haves," "could haves" and "should haves"* of your life. Life is trial and error, and you only get out of it what you put in. None of us are exempt from the process. We all miss out on opportunities and wish we could have some do-overs. There were a few stock tips I didn't take advantage of that would have made me some serious money. But no good comes of crying over spilled milk.

Before writing this book, I took a real honest look back at my life, my accomplishments and my missed opportunities. During my reflection, I also thought about legacy building and what I could do to help young people starting out in their professional lives. I wanted to do something tangible that could be a resource or roadmap for people to follow for achieving financial success and creating wealth.

After a lot of soul searching, planning and strategizing, I came up with a realistic program that I'm confident will position people for success, the **"25 to Millionaire Challenge".** It's a comprehensive approach to saving and investing that has the capacity to create wealth and prosperity. It's my hope that all who take the challenge will look back on their lives in twenty or twenty-five years and be pleased that they chose to participate. Financial stability goes a long way in this lifetime. The ability to provide and pay for everything you want and need adds quality to your life and removes some of the stress that you

155

will endure in this lifetime. You have the capacity to change the trajectory of your family.

When I was growing up in my neighborhood, we looked to athletics and entertainment for the road to riches and financial success. You don't have to be an athlete or entertainer to have a significant impact on your family or community. You don't have to know how to sing or shoot a basketball to live the life of your dreams. You just have to make the concerted effort to do the things I have spoken about all over the pages of this book. There are a million-and-one ways to amass wealth, and **the "25 to Millionaire Challenge"** is one proven method that can make you financially empowered. You may be saying, *"How do you know it's proven?"* I know because it's working for me.

Thousands claim to have a formula for financial success and the ability to make millions, but hardly any of them can provide you with authentic documentation of their success. I'm not comfortable or confident with a person telling me how to obtain something they have yet to obtain. Why would I trust someone to teach me how to be a millionaire when they are not one?

I'm not from Missouri, but I do need you to show me your success. They say experience is life's best teacher. Use my expertise and experience as an inspiration. Remember, the key elements to becoming financially empowered are sacrifice, smart and disciplined spending, consistent and realistic budgeting, living beneath your means and wise investing. If you remain committed and practice these things over and over, year after year, when you look back twenty-five years from now you will be able to see the fruits of your labor.

Today is the day to start the challenge. It will be one of the best decisions of your life. I welcome the opportunity to share my **"25 to Millionaire Challenge"** with you. Take action today by logging on at www.terrancebacchus.com. You will thank me later, but the only thanks I require is your financial success.

Your journey to becoming
financially empowered
begins today!

Bonus

Act Now

☐ Today: Accept the **25 to Millionaire Challenge**

☐ 1-3 months: Research 401(k) plans and how they work.

Prioritize Employee Benefits
When Job Searching

☐ Ask companies if they offer an employee sponsored 401(k) program and how much they contribute.

Invest First. Spend Second.

☐ Day 1 On the Job: If available, invest in your employer's retirement program (I recommend you start with 15%).

☐ Purchase life insurance. You are never too young to protect yourself.

Here Is What The Leading Experts Say

☐ 1-3 Months: Enroll in a financial seminar.

☐ 1-3 Months: Learn about IRAs.

☐ 3-6 Months: Learn about stocks, bonds, and mutual funds.

☐ 9-12 Months: Research College Savings Programs.

☐ 12-15 Months: Determine if you will self-manage your portfolio or hire an advisor or planner.

☐ When comfortable: Open up a brokerage account to start investing.

☐ 12-24 Months: Enroll in a home buying seminar.

Protect Your Assets

☐ Get a Will and obtain a Power of Attorney.

☐ Increase your life insurance to at least five times your income.

☐ Start a 529 Plan for your children.

Made in the USA
Columbia, SC
08 July 2020